Ministry of Education, Ontario
Information Centre, 13th Floor;
Mowat Block, Queen's Park,
Toronto, Ont.   M7A 1L2

HANDBOOK
For Developing Schools With Good Discipline

by

William W. Wayson
Gary G. DeVoss
Susan C. Kaeser
Thomas Lasley
Gay Su Pinnell
and the

PHI DELTA KAPPA COMMISSION ON DISCIPLINE

Phi Delta Kappa
Bloomington, Indiana

Cover design by Nancy Rinehart

Copyright © 1982 Phi Delta Kappa
All rights reserved
Library of Congress Catalogue Card Number 81-84896
ISBN 0-87367-778-1
Printed in the United States of America

Phi Delta Kappa Commission on Discipline
Ohio State University Chapter - Phi Delta Kappa

William W. Wayson, Chairperson
  Ohio State University
  Columbus, Ohio

John H. Bates
  Toronto Board of Education
  Toronto, Ontario, Canada

Rayalene Brizendine
  Southwestern School District
  Grove City, Ohio

Derek L. Burleson, PDK Liaison
  Phi Delta Kappa International
  Bloomington, Indiana

David G. Carter
  University of Connecticut
  Storrs, Connecticut

Gary G. DeVoss
  Ohio State University
  Columbus, Ohio

Susan C. Kaeser
  Citizens' Council for Ohio Schools
  Cleveland, Ohio

George Kahdy
  North Carolina State
  Department of Education
  Raleigh, North Carolina

Michael H. Kean
  Educational Testing Service
  Evanston, Illinois

Thomas Lasley
  Ohio State Department of Education
  Columbus, Ohio

Philip Lesser
  Ohio Board of Regents/AHEC
  Columbus, Ohio

Carol O'Connell
  Ohio State Department of Education
  Columbus, Ohio

Robert H. Parker
  Educational Testing Service
  Princeton, New Jersey

Pam Ptaszek
  Ohio State University
  Columbus, Ohio

Gay Su Pinnel
  Ohio State University
  Columbus, Ohio

Robert J. Rubel
  Southwest Texas State University
  San Marcos, Texas

George "Bud" Wynn
  Ohio State University
  Columbus, Ohio

Acknowledgements

This *Handbook* is the result of thousands of hours of volunteer effort by the Phi Delta Kappa Commission on Discipline members and many others too numerous to list here. Let our thanks be extended to a few that will express our appreciation to all.

Anyone familiar with modern university life will understand that the commission's work could not have been done without a supportive dean's staff at Ohio State University School of Education, so we express our deepest thanks to Bob Burnham, Don Anderson, and Russ Spillman, and to department chairperson Elsie Alberty, who made space and furniture available when the squeeze was on. We thank Linda Meadows and the staff at Ohio State University Research Foundation who administered our grant and supported our efforts. A special word of thanks goes to all of those school people who returned our extensive survey forms, which provided the raw data for this *Handbook*. We hope they will evaluate this document (whose faults are mine) as worth their effort.

The final rush to get the data analyzed and to prepare the manuscript demanded much volunteer effort because time and funds had run out. Gay Su Pinnell and her staff carried the load during the 1980 Christmas holidays, when they had much more to do. Many more days were required before the manuscript was completed. Cynthia Jackson and Theodis Fipps coded data. Pam Ptaszek performed many tasks. Barbara Hines, Betsy Greiner, and Seng Ling Chan worked overtime to get the manuscript typed, cut-and-pasted, and duplicated. Sally Lawton contributed superior typing and formating skills, and Marcella Wiseman typed free-of-charge one Saturday and Sunday. Doug Gray and his staff at Ohio State University Systems pitched in one weekend in May to clean up some very messy computer print-outs at the very last minute.

Tom Lasley, Susan Kaeser, Phil Lesser, and Gary DeVoss prepared early drafts of chapters, which were then merged into the final draft. Also Tom and Susan gave invaluable editorial advice, which helped immensely in preparing the final draft. Finally, Eva Sebo came through during the holiday season and at a time of family crisis to code over 50,000 bits of information so the computer and the authors could make sense of it. We could not have gotten here without all of their efforts.

Of course, the financial support from Phi Delta Kappa and the moral support given by the PDK Advisory Panel on Commissions and by Lowell Rose, Derek Burleson, and William Gephart of the PDK headquarters staff should be credited for our having done it at all.

William W. Wayson, Chairperson
July 1981

Table of Contents

1. Introduction and Overview........................ 1

2. What Are the Common Characteristics of
   Well-Disciplined Schools........................ 10

3. Eight Goals and a Hundred Activities for
   Developing a Well-Disciplined School.............. 29

4. The Discipline Context Inventory: A Stimulus
   for Positive Faculty Action....................... 63

5. How Can a School Get Started on Improvement...... 77

6. Conclusion and a Caution........................ 96

Bibliography....................................... 98

1
Introduction and Overview

A stable society requires citizens who are productive and know how to function independently in whatever situation they find themselves—in short, citizens who have self-discipline. They have the ability to size up a situation; see several ways of doing a task; choose one of them; do it as long as necessary or productive; and learn from the consequences.

Discipline is learned and can be taught—indeed, must be taught. One principal goal of education is to teach discipline, which is the most basic of all "basics"; none surpasses it. The challenge for educators and all adults, then, is to help children develop the skills of responsible behavior by creating an environment in which children may acquire those skills.

Unfortunately, in too many schools children do not exhibit self-discipline. They violate rules and display behavior that is not conducive to learning. Small but alarming numbers of children exhibit violent or self-destructive behavior and vandalize school property. Such negative behavior has generated great public concern about "the school discipline problem."

Viewing discipline as separate from education has often led us toward repressive measures to re-establish order rather than to provide positive educational approaches to discipline that educators know will work.

When the Phi Delta Kappa Commission on Discipline began its work in 1979, members decided to focus on school practices rather than on the socioeconomic factors that are known to affect a child's personality, expectations, values, and behavior. Such factors are not easily controlled or changed. Nevertheless, regardless of negative factors in the home, the school environment can have significant positive effects on children. Furthermore, school conditions can be more easily controlled and are more amenable to change than are the larger societal conditions. Finally, commission members were optimistic that schools could be effective institutions in developing self-disciplined children. Their task was to test that optimism.

We all know of schools where discipline does not seem to be a problem. The fact that such schools exist convinces us that solutions are possible. For this reason, the commission decided to survey schools where discipline is not seen as a problem and to approach educators in those schools in order to learn about practices that seem to assist students in becoming well-disciplined.

The results of the survey confirmed the commission's optimism. We learned about schools from all over the country, serving children from a wide range of social backgrounds, that are orderly places where children are behaving in responsible ways. That such schools exist is evidence that discipline need not be a problem and that school practices can make a great deal of difference in student behavior. This *Handbook* presents activities that have been tried in a broad sample of schools and have shown positive results. We believe that they can be implemented in any school if the staff is committed and understands the educational value of such activities.

On New Year's morning, 1981, a commentator on National Public Radio speculated that the public school system has become a decadent, perhaps antiquated, self-serving institution that is better at purveying ignorance than cultivating intelligence. The commentator predicted that rapidly developing computer and television technology, combined with new insights into how people learn and how the brain functions, could render the public schools obsolete. Despite these predictions, this *Handbook* is predicated on a belief that schools will exist for some time to come, that most students will receive the greater proportion of their formal education in schools, and that schools as we know them are not beyond repair. The experiences reported to us during the course of our study are evidence that schools in all types of communities, serving all types of students, and with no more than normal resources can provide productive and humane learning environments that will prepare self-disciplined, responsible citizens for life in the twenty-first century.

Purposes of the Study

The Phi Delta Kappa Commission on Discipline was established in 1979 to undertake a study over a 12-month period that would:

1. Identify schools that were reputed to have good discipline.
2. Survey those schools to determine what characteristics they exhibited.
3. Describe the activities in which those schools engaged to get good discipline.
4. Compile the information from the survey into a *Directory* that would help others contact the schools located by the survey.
5. Summarize the results of the survey in a *Handbook* that could guide others who wish to improve the discipline in their schools.

After eight more months of digesting the abundant information received from the survey, the results are presented in this *Handbook*, which has been compiled from an analysis of nearly 500 survey forms returned by elementary and secondary school personnel who responded to our request for information about their schools, their programs, and their communities. Through analysis of the survey forms, the commission was able to identify common characteristics among the schools and to describe the activities that they reported contributed to good discipline.

Of course, we cannot say with certainty that the activities presented in these pages will improve the discipline in any school. Indeed, for reasons discussed later in this chapter, we cannot say with certainty that the schools we surveyed are as good as they are reported to be or that they are actually doing what they reported. Nevertheless, this *Handbook* presents ideas reported by persons in nearly half a thousand schools identified by at least one knowledgeable educator as having "exemplary" discipline. The ideas are presented as suggestions that "make sense" to those of us who are experienced educators. Hopefully these suggestions will stimulate and assist school and community personnel who wish to improve discipline and productivity in their schools.

Methodology of the Study

The Commission's first task was to identify schools that were reported to have good discipline. This was done in three ways:

1. A survey of the literature yielded names and descriptions of exemplary school programs as well as the names of persons who were knowledgeable about effective schools.
2. Commission members pooled their own lists of professional

contacts and added them to the list identified through the literature search. These persons were asked to identify effective schools and a contact person at the schools. Through these methods, the commission developed a network of contacts totaling nearly 1000 persons interested in and knowledgeable about schools with effective discipline.

3. Newsletters from Phi Delta Kappa, the American Association of School Administrators, the Association for Supervision and Curriculum Development, the National Association of Secondary School Principals, and the National Association of Elementary School Principals carried announcements requesting nominations of schools with exemplary discipline.

The Commission identified more than 1000 schools. Each was sent a survey form that elicited a description of the school and its program.

Perhaps unfortunately, the commission used the phrase "schools with exemplary discipline" in its request for nominations of schools. Such a phrase undoubtedly restricted the number of schools that responded. Some respondents indicated that since they defined "exemplary" as perfect, they are unable to see themselves as fitting the description. Others were reluctant to respond to the nomination because the term "exemplary" was seen as too self-serving and might expose them to criticism. It is the commission's view that no school will ever have perfect discipline; and it is not sure that such a school would be a very good place to be. Some so-called discipline problems are healthy responses of students who need to test their environment, or to protect their self-esteem from organizational abuse, or to vent emotions that could result in far worse problems if unvented. Student misbehavior is also an excellent indicator of something going wrong in the system. So, it is doubtful that the goal of a well-disciplined school should be to eliminate *all* discipline problems.

Fortunately, over 500 schools did respond, representing all grade levels and organizational patterns, a full spectrum of urban and rural locations in the U.S. and parts of Canada, and all socioeconomic levels. Over 50,000 bits of information were coded and analyzed in an attempt to identify the practices that contributed to a particular school's reputation for having exemplary discipline.

A full description of each responding school may be found in the *Directory of Schools Reported to Have Exemplary Discipline*, published as a companion volume to this *Handbook*. The responding schools are about equally divided among urban, suburban, and rural schools and among elementary, junior high, and high schools. Every state is represented.

The commission did not try to define "good discipline" because definitions will vary depending on local conditions and values. Nor did the commission wish to impose its own concepts about discipline but rather attempted to discover what was actually occurring in schools.

Because of limited funds, time, and analytical resources, the commission did not validate the responses to see whether the schools were doing what they reported they were doing. Some schools were visited; some surveys were completed through personal interviews or through telephone interviews. Responses from schools identified in the literature were supplemented with information provided in that literature. Although some schools nominated did not seem to be examples of "exemplary discipline," and some provided too little information to make an adequate determination, commission members who reviewed the survey forms felt confident that up to 90% of the respondents deserved to be included in a list of schools with good discipline; and the practices they described were judged to be useful ways to develop good discipline in other schools.

The suggestions in this *Handbook* are drawn from responses in the surveys, from descriptions found in the literature on school discipline, and from experience of commission members. The survey form did not ask about procedures used to initiate reported practices, about the principal's role, or about change strategies. The *Handbook*, then, is a blend of practices reported by the schools and techniques supported by literature on school climate improvement, which provides good ideas for improving school discipline.

The *Handbook* was originally conceived as a publication that would describe how community relations could be a means of promoting good discipline. At the start of its work, the commission was particularly interested in discovering whether schools were finding ways to involve the community in ways that would have an effect on discipline in the school. That interest is still present. Although we discovered that many of the schools with exemplary discipline had established effective community relationships, we also discovered that good discipline in the school cannot be attributed to any one feature of the school program.

So, this *Handbook* has grown to include not only examples of good community relations but many other techniques that appear to be related to good school discipline.

There is no guarantee that any of these techniques will "work" in any given school. They seem to be working in the schools that responded to the commission's survey. But techniques cannot be lifted from one school and placed in another as auto parts can be lifted from one car and installed in another. Schools don't work that way. The success of a practice may depend very much on the particular personalities involved, a particular set of local circumstances, or a particular set of facilities or other resources. Information from the schools listed in the *Directory* clearly indicates, as we point out in Chapter 2, that certain activities when combined with certain characteristics of the school seem to result in effective discipline in those schools.

We have not tried to write a book that will account for all possible situations; we encourage our readers to use their own professional insight and adapt the suggestions offered in this *Handbook* to promote the best possible educational environment for young people in their community. If this *Handbook* stimulates that kind of activity, then the commission will have met one of its major objectives and will have fulfilled Phi Delta Kappa's ideals of leadership, research and service.

What We Started Out to Do and What We Have Done

This has been a difficult book to write. It was easy to conceive the need for such a book, but once conceived, the task itself was perplexing and elusive. Because the commission members set out to produce something *useful*, we have been supercritical of our own efforts. Each paragraph indicts itself because it cannot satisfy all those different qualities, capabilities, and resources that are found in our schools and communities. There is no recipe book for improving schools, and we know it; yet, we have had to overcome our zeal for producing one. Improving schools depends on both intuition and trained skills, which, when combined with the particular characteristics of a local school situation, lead to practices that can influence significantly the discipline climate of a school. It should be pointed out that accident and chance can also be factors that contribute to school improvements, despite nearly a century of attempts to codify and appraise the dynamics of educational change scientifically. Grasping the enormity of all these factors and presenting them in this *Handbook* was, from the beginning, a foolhardy endeavor, no matter how strong our enthusiasm was for doing it.

The desire to be scientific has also frustrated our writing this *Handbook*. Because of limited data, we were confronted time and again by the irrefutable fact that we had to go beyond the data if we were to produce anything of value for our readers. But our own research training and the sometimes excessive proscriptions imposed by research methodology tended to deter us from presenting useful information that was not always empirically proven, even though our own experience and reason convince us that such information is valid. The Man of LaMancha's insightful cry that "Facts are the enemies of Truth!" is difficult to accept when one has been trained to be concerned about sample size and statistical tests of significance to verify what are essentially commonplace and intuitive truths. We had to overcome the notion that we could support every idea or recommendation we offered by citing repeated observations from objective sources. Any effective educator has to win the same battle, else little school improvement will ever occur; for much of what passes for science in our field is more a blindfold than a lens—and all the more dangerous because it has the stamp of authority but prevents us from seeing what otherwise would be obvious.

So, this *Handbook* is not a manual or a recipe book based on scientific testing of the practices and policies we recommend. Rather, it is a careful compilation of what we found from our review of over 500 schools that seemed to have found their own ways to create exceptional programs for their students and communities. These programs in these schools are laced together with our own experience and understanding of what it takes to effect improvements in schools and other human organizations. The result, we feel, is a useful guide for educators who are dedicated to improving discipline in their schools.

The sum of the discussion is that we set out to write a recipe book; we could not do that, but we have overcome our original arrogance to produce a respectable recipe for nail soup: if you put in what you have available, you will end up with a palatable and nourishing dish that reflects the tastes and appetites of your school and community. If that occurs in several places, our nail will not have been a fraud but may indeed be seen as the horseshoe nail upon which the fate of empires depended.

Organization of the Handbook

Chapter 1 has been an introduction to the purpose of the Phi Delta Commission on Discipline, to the way in which data were collected for this *Handbook*, and to the organization of the *Handbook*.

Chapter 2, "What Are the Common Characteristics of Well-Disciplined Schools?" presents 13 characteristics that seem to prevail in the schools that were nominated as having good discipline and that replied to the commission's request for information about the schools' programs.

Chapter 3, "Eight Goals and a Hundred Activities for Improving Discipline," summarizes activities reported in the survey. Hundreds of activities reported in the survey are organized around eight general goals and categorized into 100 specific activities for improving discipline. Direct quotes from the survey forms are used to illustrate the eight general goals. Each quotation is referenced to the school from which it came so the reader can get more information either from the *Directory of Schools Reported to Have Exemplary Discipline*, the companion volume to this *Handbook*, or by contacting the school directly. The goals and activities are presented in eight tables, which can be reproduced to use with staff or community groups to stimulate thinking about alternatives they might undertake to improve school discipline.

Chapter 4, "The Discipline Context Inventory: A Stimulus for Positive Faculty Action," presents a rating form to help school staff see what needs to be done to improve discipline in the school. The *Inventory* has been used for over five years in college classes at Ohio State University and in staff development work in a dozen states. Although developed prior to our survey of schools, it closely reflects the findings of the commission's survey. The chapter also contains step-by-step instructions for using the *Inventory* to identify both strengths and problem areas in a school, and thus help the staff to begin assessing what needs to be done to develop more effective school programs.

Chapter 5, "How You Can Get Started in Your School," presents some step-by-step planning and action guides for implementing change in a local school. Much of the discussion is derived from literature and commission members' experience related to ways of bringing about change in schools. Several practical suggestions are made for ways to involve the faculty in the change process.

The bibliography is not intended to be exhaustive. It lists only a few sources a school staff might refer to for more information about action programs to improve school discipline. Sources included are those that were mentioned in survey returns or those that seemed particularly relevant for this *Handbook*.

2
What Are the Common Characteristics of Well-Disciplined Schools?

As we read the survey forms from the schools that had been nominated as having exemplary discipline, several patterns emerged from the data to give us a general portrait of schools with exemplary discipline. Although every school was different, the patterns reported here were discernible in most schools that responded to our survey.

Characteristic 1: These schools did many things that have been done by good schools and good educators for a long time.

These schools did not necessarily build their programs around unusual or innovative practices. Rather, they seemed to use an effective combination of well-known activities with a clear understanding of how the activities contributed to the total educational environment. These schools confirm that we should not dismiss practices because they have been in use for a long time. Holding award assemblies, sponsoring father-son sports events, or sending home "Happy Grams" may not at first seem so worthy of attention for dealing with discipline, which the Gallup poll has identified over the past decade as the number one problem facing the schools. Nevertheless, such activities seem to build a sense of personal pride, a sense of being a valued member of the school; and when such feelings prevail, there is less likelihood of disruptive behavior.

Characteristic 2: These schools have fostered good discipline by creating a total school environment that is conducive to good discipline rather than adopting isolated practices to deal with discipline problems.

These schools respond to discipline problems with a set of mutually supportive actions. When asked what they do about school discipline, these educators first told what they do to make their schools run effectively as educational institutions. They examined those elements of the school environment over which they had some control and then devised responses that make an orderly environment in which to teach and learn. Even when they do describe special programs or projects, a thorough examination of the total school program reveals sets of activities, which complement one another to influence discipline within the school.

An example of a coordinated, total school program is the following excerpt from the report submitted by Roy C. Ketcham High School in Wappingers Falls, N.Y.

   1. A school newsletter is sent home to parents on a monthly basis informing them of school activities, workshops, and student achievements.

   2. In the past year-and-a-half, our school has worked on a new Discipline Code. This Discipline Code was developed by a committee made up of parents, teachers, students, and administrators. After the code was developed by the committee, workshops were presented to the parents of the school district during an evening meeting; and an entire day of school was spent teaching the Discipline Code to the students. Members of the committee spent this day working with groups of 25 students, answering questions and explaining rules and regulations in the code. A workshop was also provided for the teaching staff and school monitors. At the present time we have an ongoing Review Committee made up of teachers, students, administrators, and parents to keep the Discipline Code updated and to make sure that it is being properly implemented.

   3. This year a Committee on Discipline has provided two evening workshops using guest speakers and consultants to talk about discipline. The topics for these workshops were: Strategies for Dealing with Behavior Problems in and Outside the Classroom; Study of the Total Disciplinary Process; Sharing Techniques on Solving/Preventing Discipline Problems; Techniques for Educating Parents; and Staff Effectiveness Programs.

   4. In cooperation with the art department of this high school, we have developed a program whereby students are allowed to paint murals on the walls of the halls of the schools, also mosaics and portraits. This program has not only beautified the halls of the building but has drastically cut down

on graffiti and vandalism. A local newspaper article mentioned this program.

5. In 1977-78, the school developed a strong alternative program to external suspension. Students are placed in an isolated area within the school; guidance counselors are required to visit those students within a 24-hour period after they have been placed in this room; and teachers are required to send homework to students so they do not fall behind in classroom work. This room is staffed by a certified teacher, who helps students complete work assigned to them. This teacher also makes available to those students audio-visual material on drugs, adolescent sexuality, peer pressure, etc.

6. We have a strong work-study program that allows noncollege-bound students to divide their time with school for 10 weeks and work for 10 weeks. The major subjects these students must take in order to receive a diploma are condensed into a combination English/social studies program.

7. The faculty is updated on changes in curriculum, teaching techniques, drug education, and adolescent psychology by a weekly newsletter called the "Master Teacher." The newsletter is produced within the school and placed in teachers' mailboxes every Monday morning.

8. Report cards are sent home to parents six times a year rather than four times a year as occurs in most other high schools. Report cards not only indicate the numerical grade but also indicate an effort grade and the number of days the student has been missing from a class. This report card system, while still in the experimental stage, has developed a much better communication system between school and parent.

9. A Principal's Advisory Committee made up of representatives from each department within the school meets periodically with the administrative staff to air complaints and develop new programs.

10. Students who are caught in possession of marijuana or other illegal substance are immediately arrested. At the beginning of the year, a detective from the Bureau of Criminal Identification and a New York State trooper gave workshops for all sophomores entering the school. These workshops not only explain the state laws on drugs, narcotics, and alcohol but also give students the opportunity to ask questions regarding the law. We feel that this program has greatly decreased the use of drugs in the school. Students who are arrested for possession of

drugs are suspended from school for five days and are strongly urged to participate in a local Youth Drug Abuse Program. This program is free and is staffed by a psychiatric social worker.

11. During the 1979-80 school year, this high school held a student leadership conference at a local conference center. The conference included an entire school day and evening. Students were trained in the areas of communications skills, community development, decision making, interpersonal cooperation, and goal setting. At various times during the day, students moved from one workshop to another listening to guest speakers and parents from the community, who volunteered to help. The goal of this conference was to develop student leaders, who were capable of leading committees in classrooms where student leadership was primarily needed. Many of the students that participated in this workshop will give workshops during the 1980-81 school year for other students.

12. During the 1979-80 school year, Program Teacher Advocate was developed to utilize teachers in a one-on-one program to work with students who have special discipline problems. Teachers who volunteer to work in this program meet on a weekly basis to discuss individual students who have been assigned to them. Each teacher advocate is assigned one student with whom he/she spends extra time both inside and outside the classroom. Teachers who volunteer for this program are trained by administrative personnel and guest lecturers in ways to deal with special discipline problems. Coordination with the Pupil Personnel Department is a key part of this program. This program has received adverse comments from the Teachers' Union because it is asking teachers to volunteer time without pay. This program is so new that it is hard to describe its future outcome. The goals for this program are:

- To give students an advocate teacher who will begin to know them both on an academic and personal level.
- To help students avail themselves of the various in-and out-of-school agencies that could help them and their families overcome some of the problems they are experiencing in school.
- To enable teachers to understand why discipline problems occur within the school and to help them develop new techniques for dealing with these students.

This program has never been developed at any school that I know of, and so each day is a new experience in developing the format and procedure.

Characteristic 3: Most of the educators viewed their school as a place where staff and students come to work and to experience the success of doing something well.

These educators speak often and specifically about curriculum goals, working cooperatively, and achievements accomplished. They do not separate work from human relations; rather, they base their human relations on the rewards and self-confidence that come from work well done. They are confident that the best way to create good morale, to encourage active participation, and to build self-respect is to promote the feeling of being on a winning team. They also understand that the team won't win if there isn't good communication, mutual trust, and agreed-upon purposes.

In contrast to the environment in these schools, in schools where little or nothing engaging occurs, or where little work is done, there is an atmosphere that demoralizes teachers, depersonalizes students, and stultifies enthusiasm. Poor discipline almost inevitably results from such an environment. Teachers and principals who set high expectations and help students to achieve them have good schools, because the students know what they are there to do, and they have a sense that it is important.

> Building upon basic skills developed in the elementary grades and anticipating the differentiated curriculum of the upper high grades, the program focuses upon developing each student as competent self-disciplined learner. Students learn how to learn! Students are constantly reminded in bulletins, conferences, meetings, and over the public address system that we expect excellence in all things. The successes of our students are shared with the entire student body, as are our compliments and commendations. These can be academic recognitions from outside the school, reactions of other schools or museums our students have visited, or athletic accomplishments. We have a feeling that our students *do* represent us with excellence.
> —*Fallstaff Middle School*
> *Baltimore, Md.*

The school is organized and operated along the lines of an industrial environment but with a unique and enviable managerial structure. Emphasis is on sharing responsibility

and sharing in the decision-making process. The principal is the plant manager. The shop steward is the department head, who analyzes student behavior along with the rest of the staff and makes recommendations for appropriate modifications. The students are referred to as the workers; the teacher is the foreman. The emphasis is on teaching the young men and women so that they can earn a decent living after high school. There is no short cutting of academic studies, even though the school is directed to vocational education.
— *Ossi Vocational Technical School*
Medford, N.J.

Characteristic 4: These schools are student-oriented.

This characteristic was as true for secondary as for elementary schools. The staffs did what seemed necessary for the growth of their students and for the positive image of their school. Programs were instituted for the benefit of students; and the staff served as advocates for students.

The staff works together as a unit, and all members have input into the decision-making process. Decisions are made with the thought, Is this good for children? An environment is created for children to enjoy being here and to feel free to learn and explore. This is a happy school.
— *Robins Elementary School*
Robins Air Force Base, Ga.

Principal Bill Carter and staff have emphasized that "every student has a talent." Students are taught athletic, artistic, dramatic, or musical skills. Each week features a talent assembly in which skills are practiced and demonstrated. Successes in these areas influence behavior and commitment throughout the school program. Discipline and achievement have improved markedly since the program began.
— *Mechanicsburg Elementary School*
Liberty, N.Y.

Students and their needs come first. Schedules, programs, and administrative decisions are based on what is best for the students, not what is best for the administration and staff. There is excellent rapport between our staff and students. Our students realize that staff is genuinely interested in them. This

is aided by one-to-one contacts in the learning centers. We have a very active and comprehensive extracurricular program that shows a positive interest by our staff and offers educational benefits to our students.
—*Pompton Lakes High School*
Pompton Lakes, N.J.

Characteristic 5: These schools focused on causes of discipline problems rather than symptoms.
Educators in well-disciplined schools know that behavior is caused. When misbehavior occurred, the principal and faculty tended to go beyond merely punishing students for the misbehavior. They searched for probable causes, and they addressed them. They improved discipline in their schools by taking steps to remove those causes and by establishing activities within their school and community that would result in good behavior.

Our respondents did not present a list of punishments to control student behavior; they did not define problems in terms of individual student behavior. Instead they looked at student behavior as a symptom of other problems. By looking beyond individual symptoms, by avoiding simple explanations, they were able to devise activities that truly improved student behavior.

Table 1 illustrates how three schools in our survey related their disciplinary efforts to organizational factors, staff attitudes, parent attitudes, curriculum, or interpersonal relationships, which they felt were the causes for student misbehavior.

Characteristic 6: Programs in these schools emphasized positive behaviors and used preventive measures rather than punitive actions to improve discipline.
The surveys repeatedly contained descriptions of ways to reward positive behavior. Awards, honor days, positive messages to parents, praise, recognition through publicity, photographs, or lists posted in prominent places in the school, lunches with teachers or principals, prizes, trips or privileges earned by accumulating points for positive behavior—all these and more were cited as reasons for a school's good discipline.

It seems clear that the success of these schools is not related to their having *either* restrictive or permissive rules but rather to the degree to which their procedures were communicated and accepted as being fair and well-intended. A good proportion of the

TABLE 1
SYMPTOMS OF DISCIPLINE PROBLEMS IN THREE SCHOOLS AND ACTIVITIES INSTITUTED TO DEAL WITH REAL CAUSES

Location	Symptoms	Causes	Activities Instituted
RCA School Youth Development Center, Cornwell Heights, Pa.	Verbally abusing teachers	Lack of respect for students and their culture	Established leadership that would not tolerate unsirable behavior
	Physically abusing teachers	High unemployment	Established a policy of respect for students, staff, and property
	Lack of respect for authority	Poor housing	Instituted a new curriculum with strong supervision of students' learning
	Vandalism	Racism	Established a policy of students sharing power and authority
	Students verbally and physically abusive to each other	School apathy	Hired the best qualified staff available
	Drugs out of control	Poorly trained staff	Eliminated the policy of suspensions and expulsions
	Student absenteeism	Student and staff absenteeism	
Eagle Grove Community High School, Eagle Grove, Ia.	Extensive vandalism of school property	Lack of involvemnt	Written rules with definite consequences for infractions
	Disrespect for people	Lack of rules for attendance and discipline	Staff coordination and cooperation
	Falling test scores	Lack of follow-up on disruptive behavior	Consistent enforcement of rules and regulations

Eagle Grove continued page 18

TABLE 1. continued

Location	Symptoms	Causes	Activities Instituted
	Student disinterest in school	Staff not working together	Better supervision in all areas
	Lack of school spirit	Extensive exceptions made to rules	Strict enforcement of passes into and out of classrooms
	Lack of student participation in school activities	Leadership inconsistent	Support of staff by administration
		Limited activities in community	Communications and meetings with parents
		Staff primarily concerned with self-preservation	Student handbook
		Parent apathy and disinterest	News articles on policies and practices
Wyatt High School, Ft. Worth, Texas	Fighting, threatening, bullying, and other behavior that contributed to an unpleasant atmosphere	Racial myths and stereotypes prevalent. Blacks and whites did not trust each other and students believed the other race to be responsible for past and present misfortunes.	We brought the leaders of all student groups together and made them listen to one another.
			After listening, we had a retreat on a Friday evening and all day Saturday at which students participated in activities that caused changes in their attitudes.

schools had developed behavior codes for dealing with specific infractions. Even those schools that had rather rigid rules seemed to project an atmosphere of caring and concern for students. However, very few schools concentrated their discipline efforts on enforcing rules and meting out punishment. Most engaged in a wide range of practices designed to establish norms of conduct and then to gain widespread commitment to live by those norms.

One important factor, if not the most important, in any discipline plan is the positive reinforcers for good behavior. As a building, we are stressing verbal praise and the sending of positive notes home. We also have a monthly "Good Guy Movie" for those students who have faithfully observed the behavior guidelines set by their teachers. The movies are feature films purchased by the PTA. Each teacher has developed positive reinforcement strategies. Some use an "honor roll" system, others drop marbles into a jar when they see appropriate behavior. Each of these methods results in a positive consequence when a goal has been reached. Notes are sent home from the principal, with a new twist. Entitled, "Your Child Was Sent to the Principal Today," the note describes the child's good behavior that earned the right to go to the principal's office.
—*Lee Elementary School*
Richland, Wash.

Schools are positive places—places for students, parents, and teachers. No one group can run the school without the others. I'm very proud of this school. What we have built here is a place where students come to learn and behave and still enjoy it; where teachers are proud to be employed; and parents are satisfied with what they have.
—*Seymour Elementary School*
Payson, Ill.

We stress preventive programs. Usually schools deal with *symptoms* of problems, not the causes. When there is a lack of communication between staff and students, the student has less reason to believe he is responsible. When students are not accepted or trusted, they are frustrated; and you will have bad behavior. You cannot just insist that students behave; teachers and other staff must work closely with students to help them see

what behaving means. We use social studies, for example, to deal with causes to help students learn how to handle themselves and to understand procedures, other than fighting, for solving interpersonal problems.
— *Rocky Mountain Elementary School*
Marietta, Ga.

We at Beta School believe in positive reinforcement. Commendation Cards are issued freely and warmly. Progress, however slight, is lavishly commended. Our students have been subjected to negative correction for years, and there has been no improvement. They must be convinced that they are not "losers."

One of our teachers used the positive approach to solve a homework problem in her sixth-grade class. The first homework assignment was completed by only 2 of 12 students. The teacher praised the two highly, gave them extra credit and Commendation Cards, and inscribed their names on the Sixth-Grade Hall of Fame Roster. The next homework assignment was completed by five students. In one week's time, homework was being completed by an average of nine students daily. Now that the vast majority was functioning well, the teacher could now be a little more strict with the delinquent minority.
— *The Beta School**
District 4, New York City

*A school for underachieving boys and girls who have difficulty adjusting to the regular school.

One has to look beyond the language often used in discussions about discipline, because the speaker's own actions belie the language, which often is negative, punitive, and restrictive. H. Lloyd Cooper, the director of secondary education in the Warren Township (Indiana) School Corporation, sent us the text of a speech in which he made the no-nonsense assertion that:

The time is overdue for a more authoritative educational voice in the permissive wilderness of our society . . . . One of our goals should be a plan of action to return high schools to a safe, serene, learning situation, as free of student vandalism, violence, or disruption as possible. A concerted effort should be made . . . by enforcing the rules of the school and thus preventing disorder and disruption of the learning process.

But his call for "law and order" advised in equally no-nonsense terms:

> To enforce the rules and to improve the educational climate of our schools would be to take a giant step toward humanizing our schools. Bold action taken by a comprehensive, all inclusive, supervisory staff team which expands the freedom of each individual student by fairly, firmly, and kindly enforcing the rules (via due process) can vastly improve the living and learning atmosphere of a high school.
>
> Simply to improve the custodial safety of incarcerated young people is not enough . . . Plan ways to let the students enjoy more fully the freedoms . . . . The staff should be motivated to provide an imaginative, creative, active, diversified, educational program . . . . When imaginative curricular and extracurricular innovations take place in an educational arena where all necessary rules are enforced, the results are most gratifying.

Thus, even seeming hardliners may be advocating a positive and supportive school environment as a means of attaining good discipline.

> We preach and practice a very strong code of discipline. We square up to every issue and take the offensive. We believe in strong administrative leadership, a code of conduct for students and fair enforcement of that code. We hold students liable for all damages if there are any. We promote the feeling that everybody (teachers, parents, and students) is important. Our desire is to fulfill our educational commitment to prepare youngsters properly for adult life.
> —*Hayes Junior High School*
> *Youngstown, Ohio*

Characteristic 7: These schools adapted practices to meet their own identified needs and to reflect their own styles of operation.

Very few schools reported that their discipline programs were based on any of the widely publicized programs for improving discipline. Those that were reported were mentioned only a few times and included *Teacher Effectiveness Training, Discipline Without Tears, Reality Therapy, Assertive Discipline, School Climate Improvement, Transactional Analysis, Project PASS,* an approach used by the Institute for Effective Integrated Education at Ohio State University, and Madeline Hunter's motivation curriculum. (See full references in the bibliography.) A few schools reported using behavior modification approaches but named no particular plan. However, many schools did use positive reward techniques. Even those schools that did identify particular programs reported that they modified the practices to fit their own circumstances.

Ferndale Junior High School in High Point, N.C., reported how its program evolved over several years:

> It began in 1976 with an in-depth study of our school rules. The rules were rewritten and reorganized. Students had to sign that they had been taught and understood the rules. Each year we do that.
>
> After some members of the staff participated in workshops dealing with William Glasser's reality therapy, we began to develop the Ferndale Student Management System based on his "10 steps." Two staff members visited Northbrook High School in Houston where they had been using the Glasser model for five years. They recommended our using the Houston system with changes to fit our needs.
>
> Two other staff members visited Project PASS in St. Petersburg, Fla. We then had a PASS workshop for seven of our staff. Those seven had a session with the rest of the staff on humanistic activities. Then the whole school system participated in the same activities.
>
> The program developed by our school is called *The Ferndale Student Management System*, or *Ferndale: A Good Place to Be*. The staff evaluates the program each spring and changes take place with staff development activities each August. The idea is based on Glasser; however, we have incorporated other ideas and concepts also.

Characteristic 8: The principal plays a key role in making these schools what they are.

No single person has as much impact on the discipline climate of a school as does the principal. When the impact is negative, and it sometimes is, we might wish that the staff would take more responsibility for creating better learning environments. But when the impact is positive, and the mix is right, and the school seems to be excellent, the principal's influence is usually the determining factor.

I started teaching with Greg Caras as my principal. He is still there at Longfellow School making the school a topnotch place. He demanded that we get off our buns and do things we thought impossible. I remember him saying to me many times when I told him I could not do something, "Now I *know* you can do it and I know that you will." By golly, every time, don't you know, I did it? I never learned as much in my life.
—*Longfellow Elementary School
Dayton, Ohio*

Last year, before Mr. Martin came here, it was a disaster. In just a few months, he has turned the whole school around. Look how excited the staff is! No kids in the hall raising hell anymore! He really has made a difference. Of course, desegregation helped a little, and he brought in his whole team, Stephie and Bones, (vice principals) with him and they work together like clockwork.
—*A. B. Hart Junior High School
Cleveland, Ohio*

Everybody knows "Pops" Miller. He *is* that school. He knows his kids can do right, and he sees that they do it. They are all his kids. He talks about retiring, but I don't know what he would do or what the school would do without him.
—*East Mecklenburg High School
Charlotte, N.C.*

Fred Aeillo had to retire and go to Texas this year. He was so dedicated to his schools, and he made a difference in everyone of them even though the district was against him all the way much of the time. He used to demand more of us teachers than we thought we could give, but don't you know, we could do it. Raper School will never be the same without him, nor will any other school he ever worked with.
—*Raper Elementary School
Cleveland, Ohio*

Characteristic 9: The programs in these schools often result, either through happy coincidence or through deliberate design, from the teamwork of a capable principal and some other staff member who has the personal leadership qualities that complement those of the principal.

This informal leadership team combines the authority of a strong principal with the determination and skills of a task-oriented lieutenant. The roles may be reversed; the principal may provide the instructional leadership and the lieutenant attends to the interpersonal and public relations requirements. But the combination is an unbeatable one and may be the true key to the principal's success. It may also explain why some principals fail when they leave a successful school and assume duties in another school minus the complementary lieutenant.

> During 1972, Dolores Perez, the Intensive Reading Improvement Program (IRIP) teacher at Ericson, attended two weeks of special training on Continuous Progress. She became very interested in the program and took it on as a special mission . . . . She and several other teachers began to put together a set of guidelines for implementing Continuous Progress, to translate the philosophy into action . . . . When Miss Branch (the principal) arrived in May 1973, she and Dolores Perez became a team. The pace really stepped up. Together they put together a manual for implementing Continuous Progress at Ericson School . . . . Dolores Perez had the support of the Ericson teachers. She was popular, a hard worker, and "one of them." She dedicated herself to implementing the Continuous Progress program, and as a result of her success, she was promoted . . . . One teacher reported that the only negative critical incident she could think of since Miss Branch arrived was when Dolorez Perez left Ericson . . . . It has been a period of intense creative growth.
> —*Leif Ericson Elementary School*
> *Chicago, Ill.* (taken from a report to the school board 8 April 1979)

Characteristic 10: The staffs of these schools believe in their school and in what its students can do; and they expend unusual amounts of energy to make that belief come true.

No person alone can make a good school. Even though the principal's role is key, the staff has to be willing and able to make it work. Principals who returned surveys generally attributed much of their school's success to "an extraordinary staff." Their supportive behavior makes the program a reality. Then they sell the program with enthusiasm to the community—and in several cases to the teacher unions. Often they risk censure from fellow professionals in their school or school district. Their positive belief and enthusiasm create an atmosphere in the school that is contagious. They surround the students with programs and activities, which make them want to contribute and to become a part of what is going on.

> We are a family now. We work together, believe in one another and know this can be a good school. It is a whole new world for us.
> —*A. B. Hart Junior High School*
> *Cleveland, Ohio*

> We had to overcome many deficiencies in the building to provide an adequate program. Although the school is still inadequate in many ways, it is because of the quality and determination of the faculty that the school is able to provide an excellent program for its students.
> —*Appollo High School*
> *Owensboro, Ky.*

> A highly motivated faculty has produced a highly motivated student body. The emphasis upon assuming responsibility and sharing in the decision-making process is passed on to the students.
> —*Ossi Vocational Technical*
> *High School*
> *Medford, N.J.*

Characteristic 11: Teachers in these schools handle all or most of the routine discipline problems themselves.

The principal and counselors handle serious cases, but the authority and responsibility is firmly established for the teacher to deal with routine discipline cases. The school provides support for teachers' actions. When teachers employ poor practices, they can get help to improve them and are expected to do so.

The staff works exceptionally well together and has a very positive and concerned attitude toward the students and fellow teachers. The teachers assume and handle the majority of the discipline problems that arise. This is done in a very positive and consistent manner. Our strength lies in the attitude developed between the teachers and students, school, and community. We believe in a positive, hard working approach toward school. We put trust in our students and staff and expect that the trust be kept. Community support has come from the development of this trust and confidence in our ability to "get the job done."
—*Jouette Middle School*
Albermarle County, Va.

Our school has been successful due to its Behavioral Teacher Approach in which discipline is dealt with at the teacher level as opposed to the main office level. We have a special behavioral room, which provides for constructive interaction between teacher and student. Discipline is viewed from a developmental viewpoint and is accomplished by incorporating discipline as part of the academic program.
—*Marblehead Junior High School*
Marblehead, Mass.

Characteristic 12: The majority of these schools have developed stronger-than-average ties with parents and with community agencies.

Going beyond the usual infrequent and perfunctory relationships, these schools sought active ties with the home and with other community institutions.

Our Planning/Leadership Team allows community members to have input in decision making, in setting goals, in establishing budgets, and in dealing with other districtwide concerns.
—*Ferndale Junior High School*
High Point, N.C.

Our court-ordered partnership with the Port Authority gives rise to many positive relationships, including an all-sport awards banquet. The school has developed close relationships with the business world to discuss problems and to establish a Flexible Campus Program for job placement. Parents and

community members are involved in developing an open house, in developing discipline procedures for the school, in determining scholarship winners, and in having community leaders lecture and give advice.
—*East Boston High School*
Boston, Mass.

The school building is used by so many churches and community groups that there are few nights when the building is empty. The cafeteria is open, and parents can drop in for lunch and visits. The guidance department and administration work so closely with parents that they feel free to ask for and get advice and help concerning their children and family. One third of the half-dozen organizations that meet each night have school personnel as presidents or other key members.
—*Smithfield Junior High School*
Smithfield, N.C.

Characteristic 13: These schools were open to critical review and evaluation from a wide variety of school and community sources.

Staff, parents, students, and often community agencies were welcomed into the school for a variety of informal contacts, and they were listened to, although not slavishly obeyed. Most of the schools reported annual or other reviews of their practices, with provisions to revise and to retrain staff to implement the revisions. Both formal policy-making and advisory groups were mentioned in many survey returns; and all combinations of staff, students, parents, and community members participated in these groups. Very few of these groups seemed to be "window dressing"; and none were reported as being hostile to the school's efforts, presumably because there was a genuine attempt to listen to and to respond to them. The staff responded to problems by trying to solve them.

We invite parents to visit school at any time. We want an open climate. Since we are proud of what we are doing, we welcome all parents.
—*Hayes Junior High School*
Youngstown, Ohio

Students are included on every committee from curriculum to the parent-teacher-student association. Parents serve on

Curriculum and Textbook Advisory Committee and also serve on an Advisory Committee to the principal.
— *Warren Central High School*
Indianapolis, Indiana

The students interview all prospective staff members before they are hired.
— *RCA School Youth Development Center*
Cornwells Heights, Pa.

A decentralized decision-making model allows parents and teachers to work directly to achieve instructional goals. Parents are involved in most aspects of school operation, including developing policies governing discipline, minimum standards of achievement, and the hiring of staff.
— *Windsor Elementary School*
St. Louis, Mo.

The principal has evening hours for parents every other Tuesday; and all parents are invited to the school on a rotating basis for coffee, questions, and input. The school also sponsors evening programs for parents that deal with situations which parents see as problems.
— *Greenfield Junior High School*
Greenfield, Mass.

Summary

Certain patterns emerge from our review of the surveys from schools reputed to have good discipline. The picture shows schools with closer-than-average ties to home and community, doing things advocated by educational theorists for many years. They attempt to identify causes for discipline problems and respond by creating a total school environment to achieve worthwhile educational purposes. A strong principal with a dedicated and energetic staff share in making decisions on what is good for students. They stress high expectations and offer positive reinforcement for individual achievement. Staff and students seem self-confident and proud of the achievements in their school. They seem to be models of professional self-discipline.

3
Eight Goals and a Hundred Activities for Developing a Well-Disciplined School

Literally thousands of specific activities were reported as "working" in the communities and schools that responded to our survey. They demonstrate what creativity, commitment, enthusiasm, and energy can accomplish; they represent a catalogue of alternative ways to reduce discipline problems, which may help other schools and communities as they set out to develop well-disciplined schools.

No school was doing all of the activities, so we have put together a composite of the activities to describe an idealized but nonexistent school. In deciding to implement any of these activities, educators should keep in mind local circumstances, but they can be assured that *some schools somewhere* have used these practices successfully. Whether or not they will be successful in a new situation will depend, of course, on the skill with which the school staff can adapt them to new circumstances. The commission does not recommend that schools adopt a practice "lock, stock and barrel," and then expect to "plug it in." Too much has been done already to standardize American schools; that in itself is a major cause for disruptive, undisciplined behavior.

For more detailed information about the practices described in this chapter, the commission recommends contacting the schools. The school addresses and a contact person are listed in the *Directory of Schools Reported to Have Exemplary Discipline*, the companion volume to this *Handbook*. When making such contacts, with the intent of adopting certain practices, educators should keep the following points in mind:

1. The program may no longer be in existence at the time of

the contact or visit. Even so, it would be a mistake to reject the idea simply because it is now defunct.

2. Persons involved in programs may not really be aware of what made them succeed or fail. Their descriptions may overlook critical factors that are necessary in making it work in another school. Be alert to qualities that are essential to the success of the program but are not easily transported to another school and to important problems that may not have been reported.

3. Even the best programs have some problems. If the program is not perfect or isn't functioning perfectly on a day that you visit the school, don't let this distract you from the many advantages the program does offer.

4. People who describe (or observe) practices in schools have many reasons for judging a program to be good (or bad) other than its effect on students. Don't let another person's biases influence what you see and what you adopt or what you reject.

To make the best use of this *Handbook,* keep in mind that your school is unique, and you are unique. The *Handbook* will not provide ready-made remedies for the problems you experience. But it does provide a wealth of ideas that have worked in other schools. You can examine and appraise them, and then decide if and how they might be adapted to help solve problems in your school. Your knowledge of the human and material resources available, your ability to enlist others to make the program work, and your enthusiasm about the program are the critical ingredients for success. With these ingredients, you can make anything work; without them, any program will fail.

Eight Goals for a Well-Disciplined School

Our survey of well-disciplined schools turned up a variety of activities or programs, which we have organized under eight goals. As we analyzed the returns, many activities seemed to serve more than one goal. For example, an activity we placed under the goal of *increasing students' sense of belongingness* might also logically fall under the goals of *reducing status differences* or *strengthening relationships with the homes* or *enhancing curriculum and instruction.* Thus, many educational practices serve many goals at the same time, thereby increasing the internal consistency and unity of the total program.

In the remainder of this chapter we shall discuss how each of these eight goals relates to school discipline, and then we present both general and specific activities that were reported on our surveys. In doing so, we try to blend specific, practical ideas with the reasons for doing them, so as to stimulate the reader to apply the ideas most effectively to his or her own situation and circumstance.

Goal 1. *To improve the way in which people in the school work together to solve problems.*

Schools that wish to teach students self-discipline must have a staff with a shared sense of purpose and a commitment to do what is necessary to achieve that purpose. Both students and staff must understand what the school is trying to do and must feel personally responsible for seeing that it is done well. They must feel a sense of ownership and pride in the school and must continuously work to enhance it.

Good schools involve the staff in the total life and operation of the school. When the teacher's role is so circumscribed that important professional responsibilities are delegated to someone else, the result is a loss of confidence, status, and professional prestige. Morale, interest, and productivity decrease. Many schools in our survey emphasized teachers' involvement in decision making, in making comprehensive plans for school improvement, and in participating in activities outside the classroom. The following are a few examples:

> We ended the year by asking the school staff to identify the 10 greatest strengths and the 10 areas in need of most attention. They began a continuous process to develop and improve the school.
> —*Parkview Junior High School*
> *Mukwonago, Wisc.*

> Staff meetings are used for "self-evaluation," evaluating the administration, and mutual problem solving. Staff members make a point of coming early enough to spend a few minutes with their colleagues before school. Administrators set aside an hour before and after school when they will be available to talk with individuals or groups of teachers.
> —*Brookside Elementary School*
> *Waterville, Maine*

Our school has several ways of creating staff cohesion. A hospitality committee serves refreshments at staff meetings and plans a potluck luncheon and breakfast each year. The staff also has "secret pals" who remember each other on special occasions throughout the year.
—*Cash Elementary School*
Kernersville, N.C.

Good schools are dynamic staff training institutions, with programs to help the staff develop skills in working together to solve the problems that affect job satisfaction and the overall operation of the school. Informal meetings are frequent. Formal staff development sessions are designed for specific purposes that are clearly related to improving the school. Staff development is regarded as one of the most important activities in the school, second only to student instruction.

First identifying problems and then doing something about them is a way of life in good schools. Refusing to be overwhelmed by the sheer number of problems needing attention, the staff sets priorities, assigns tasks, and sets deadlines. As each problem is successfully solved, it generates the will to work on new ones. With success comes the self-confidence to share problems and resolve them instead of hiding them for fear of being criticized. Criticism is accepted as well-intended in order to solve problems affecting the school.

The principal's style of leadership seems to be an important factor in getting a staff to work together to solve problems. Friendly, open, encouraging behavior seems to bring out the best in the staff. Principals who are visible in the hallways, cafeterias, and on the playground set an example for the staff. The principal attends staff development sessions and takes something from the experience and relates it back to day-to-day operations. The principal articulates the school's goals and works with the staff to achieve those goals. The principal accepts criticism and gives it when needed. The principal welcomes leadership from the staff and gives credit for the contributions of others.

Table 2 presents objectives and activities that help staff work together to solve problems.

Goal 2. *To reduce authority and status differences among all persons in the school.*

Self-discipline, by definition, implies responsible behavior. Responsible behavior is an internalized commitment to do what

TABLE 2

OBJECTIVES AND ACTIVITIES FOR IMPROVING THE WAY SCHOOL STAFF WORK TOGETHER TO SOLVE PROBLEMS

Objectives	*Activities*
To improve the quality of teaching and learning.	Involve staff in defining goals and purposes.
To develop a mutual sense of purpose among staff.	Continuously translate goals into actions.
To improve communication and problem-solving skills among staff.	Involve staff in making decisions about school policy.
To increase staff responsibility for decision making in the school.	Involve staff in curriculum planning.
To increase understanding of and commitment to decisions that have been made.	Improve informal staff interaction to make the school more like a family or community.
To increase staff motivation and pride.	Improve faculty meetings, making them problem-solving sessions rather than information-giving or "gripe" sessions.
To give staff new challenges and choices.	Establish schedules to allow planning time.
To improve staff skills in dealing with new situations and new problems.	Eliminate unnecessary tasks so staff has cooperative planning time.
To enable staff to be supportive of and supported by professional colleagues.	Focus on concern for students.
To provide feedback to staff on methods for improving school operations.	Have the principal assist in classrooms.
To provide staff with administrative models for professional behavior.	Train staff to communicate and problem-solve together.
	Improve supervision by giving specific feedback. Involve staff in self analysis of school and classroom problems.
	Enable staff members to observe one another at work.
	Enable staff members to interact with personnel from other schools.
	Send staff on field trips, retreats, or to professional meetings.

one has agreed to do without outside coercion. The best discipline programs try to generate that kind of internal commitment by giving individuals the opportunity to participate in the decisions that affect them.

Strong authority differences generally deny staff and students the opportunity to make decisions. Indeed, authoritarian decision making generally gives persons reasons for thinking that the problems in the school are someone else's and that they have no responsibility for their solution. Research by Stanley Milgram shows that people feel little responsibility—even for inhumane actions—when authority figures (or the "system") assume responsibility for what happens.* If solutions to problems come exclusively from an authoritarian figure, the staff and students may feel no responsibility at all for making them work and may even consciously or unconsciously work to make them fail, depending upon the personal allegiance that is felt toward the authoritarian person who initiated the solution. By broadening the participation in problem solving, a school staff will contribute to the solution and feel responsible for carrying it out. Similarly, students who are involved in problem solving will take more responsibility for seeing that school problems are reduced.

Sharp status differences also create tensions, negative attitudes, and frustrations that lead to undesirable behavior. People who are treated as lower status feel they are not as valued and are in some ways "inferior." They often respond by doing something to protect their egos; and what they do is sometimes seen as a discipline problem. Whether it is a custodian who is treated as a menial, or a "traveling teacher" who serves two schools so is not included in faculty social activities, or a vocational teacher in an academically-oriented high school whose subject area is seen as second-rate, or a student who is labeled a misfit in the school—any of these persons may become a discipline problem, either by withdrawing contributions, by turning their allegiance outside the organization, by stirring up opposition to the school, by being disruptive and hard to handle, or by turning the status system around and trying to prove that others are "more inferior than I am."

Good schools tend to involve the staff and even the students and outsiders in decision making. They take steps to reduce

---

*Stanley Milgram, *Obedience to Authority* (New York: Harper and Row) 1974.

sharp status differences that cause irresponsible behavior. Traditional job titles, departmental in-groups, and geographic or personal differences are bridged by various formal and informal means designed to open communications and to mobilize the resources necessary to make the school better.

Staff members in such schools worry less about whose job it is and spend less time blaming someone else for not taking care of the situation. They don't depend on authority figures or "they" to solve the school's problems; they set out to do what needs doing by using their own initiative and ingenuity to persuade others, to secure resources, to organize action, and to assess results. Such staffs tolerate criticism from one another without becoming defensive. Because they have had many successes to give them confidence, they try things that might fail, because they know they can learn from failure how to do it better next time. Because noncertified staff and students are valued and included in planning, they are more willing to contribute to the general operation of the school. They also share available resources because they trust one another and don't need to protect what is "theirs."

Schools in the survey reported many activities that reduce status and authority differences. Here are some illustrations:

> The word "staff" refers to all adults who work on a regular basis in the building regardless of titles or job descriptions. Staff members believe that each member of the staff serves as a "role model" for some children in the building.
> —*Franklin Elementary School*
> *St. Louis, Mo.*

> Shared decision making is a major goal of our program. The school engages in schoolwide decision making, involving both staff and students. Task forces are established to deal with critical school issues such as curriculum design, communication, inservice, and discipline.
> —*West Junior High School*
> *Colorado Springs, Colo.*

> Our staff has instituted intensive staff development following an examination of how different teaching styles interact with student learning styles to foster learning or to create problems. The inservice is offered by local experts. The training has reduced undesirable behaviors markedly.
> —*Marblehead High School*
> *Marblehead, Mass.*

Table 3 presents objectives and activities that help schools reduce nonproductive divisions among staff and among students.

TABLE 3

OBJECTIVES AND ACTIVITIES THAT REDUCE AUTHORITY AND STATUS DIFFERENCES AMONG ALL PERSONS IN THE SCHOOL

Objectives	*Activities*
To get commitment from staff and students to participate in problem solving and to implement decisions.	Stress the goal of teaching all students.
To foster coesion among all who work together in the school.	Create instructional groupings that bring students together.
To have the school program serve all who work together in the school.	Create many ways for success so that all students have a chance to be successful.
To involve more people in the life the school.	Display all student work, not just that of the "good" students.
To maximize support for school programs.	Eliminate requirements that block participation in extracurricular activities.
To use all of the available ideas and resources that people in the school have in their possession.	Have students share in solving school and classroom problems.
To reduce barriers to communication.	Involve staff, students, and parents in decision making.
	Have staff and students work together on projects and share recognition.
	Establish formal student/faculty groups.
	Have staff/student social events.
	Involve staff and students who are hesitant to participate.
	Develop a "Bill of Rights" for all people in the school.

Table 3 continued page 37

TABLE 3 continued

Objectives	Activities
	Structure decision-making groups across departmental and grade divisions.
	Give recognition to all staff, both certified and noncertified.
	Involve both certified and non-certified personnel in faculty meetings.
	Have staff members run faculty meetings.
	Go out of your way to get all staff at social events.
	Welcome all parents.

Goal 3. *To increase and widen students' sense of belonging in the school.*

Students will take more responsibility for behaving appropriately if they feel that the school is theirs. Students who are involved in the school, who feel that the school is a safe and happy place to be, and who feel that they are valued in the school are not likely to be discipline problems. Students who help to make decisions about the school, who do some of the work to keep it functioning smoothly, and who participate in activities feel that they have a stake in the place.

Staff members who know their students by name and show interest in them outside the classroom are showing respect for their students and their families. When students are treated impersonally and have no interaction with staff members except "on business," they feel little obligation to make the school work better. When no one will listen to their side of a problem, when they are punished for things they did not do and have no recourse, when they have no one on the staff who will protect their interests or give them help when they can't do the work, they feel no sense of responsibility for what happens in the school. With such feelings, it is little wonder that they become disruptive.

Having a personal contact on the staff and a "home base" within the school organization seems to be an important factor in determining whether students are self-disciplined or whether they will require continuous adult supervision. Good schools are organized to assure some personal contact among students and staff members, either through self-contained classrooms, homeroom periods, or a system of advisors, "buddies," "big brothers," or even volunteer grandparents. Such schools also try to improve personal contacts. They know students by name. They eliminate huge impersonal study halls. They use personal ways to welcome students to school and avoid huge assemblies and massive "troop movements" that characterize many large secondary schools on opening day.

Student involvement in school activities seem to be another key to good school discipline. Good schools have a wide choice of extracurricular activities to serve the interests of larger numbers of students. Other avenues of student involvement that promote responsibility include Glasser circles (see William Glasser's *Schools Without Failure*), active student councils, and principal's student advisory groups, all of which can provide student opportunities for resolving real school problems. Having responsible jobs, such as cleaning up or beautifying the facilities, or serving on a "welcome team" to greet new students on opening day, gives students an important role in the life of the school.

Students often can be the catalyst for improving a classroom or a school. Ted Urich and Robert Batchelder describe in "Turning an Urban High School Around," (*Phi Delta Kappan*, November 1979) how one school worked through students to overcome the urban high school syndrome—absenteeism, tardiness, apathy, tension, six principals in six years, low staff morale, low achievement, and bad reputation.

Seventy students and a dozen teacher-volunteers participated in a weekend of leadership training at a free facility at a local college. Training was provided in problem solving, feedback communication, conflict resolution, decision making, parliamentary procedure, change strategy, action planning, and team building. Total cost: $600 and it could have been done for less.

The school has turned around and is moving positively. The training is now an annual event, and participation has doubled. Any school faculty with a will could do the same thing. The authors advise:

- Improving a school doesn't cost a lot of money.
- The whole staff doesn't have to be convinced; a dedicated few can initiate it.
- Leadership training is a continuing activity, not a one-shot affair.

- Trust students to make decisions that will improve the school.

When students are invited to participate in solving such problems as drug trafficking, poor facilities, noisy halls, or dirty cafeterias; and when they are given procedures to carry out their decisions, they are learning the skills of responsible, effective citizenship. By involving students in solving real problems in the school, they can see that such problems are a problem for all people in the school and not just for the professional staff.

If students can see the staff as real people, they are more likely to feel that they are part of the school family. Interacting with teachers or other staff on camping trips, at informal lunches, in hallway discussions, or on the playground helps students see their teachers as people with feelings and with interests beyond their roles in the formal classroom. Such contacts prevent both staff and students from falling into a "them vs. us" syndrome. Good schools create opportunities for staff and students to see one another as people through such practices as faculty/student athletic contests, beautification projects, community service projects, and a variety of extracurricular activities.

A number of schools in our survey reported on ways of getting more students involved in the life of the school. Many junior high and high schools have special days to spark school spirit: Grandparents Day, Color Days, Dress-up Day, Dress-down Day, Switch Day, and many more. T-shirts, buttons, jackets, hats, pennants, and other symbols are extensively used to rally school spirit and increase student involvement. The major goal is to help students feel that they "belong" to the school, that the school "belongs" to them, and that the school is worth "belonging to."

> Our philosophy is to get everyone involved. We have a separate cheerleading squad for each varsity team, thus involving a total of 56 different cheerleaders. There are enough extracurricular activities to involve most of the students. Students who are cut from the varsity and junior varsity basketball team compose a "B" basketball team, which has its own coach and plays its own schedule of games. We encourage wide participation in all extracurricular activities and attempt to implement a policy of "catching students doing good things and then rewarding them for their accomplishments."
> —*Rocky River High School*
> *Rocky River, Ohio*

We reduced discipline problems by giving students more responsibility in the school. A big brother and big sister program pairs older students with younger ones to give assistance both academically and socially. Teachers are available one-and-a-half hours during the day and for one hour after school for tutoring individual students. A wide range of extracurricular activities are offered and students have opportunity for a field trip every month. (The school custodian wrote that the students love the school and the yearly vandalism cost is less than $25.00).
—*Garfield School*
Revere, Mass.

Our program emphasizes school spirit by having a school mascot, and a "Purple and White" group who paint their faces and cheer at athletic events, "Bleacher Creatures" (a student pep club), special talent shows, open houses, and student productions.
—*New Ulm High School,*
New Ulm, Minn.

Table 4 lists several objectives and activities for helping students to feel that their school "belongs" to them.

TABLE 4

OBJECTIVES AND ACTIVITIES FOR HELPING STUDENTS GAIN A SENSE OF BELONGINGNESS IN THEIR SCHOOL

Objectives	*Activities*
To increase students' sense of "belonging" in the school.	Involve students in making decisions about the operation of the school, e.g., student council, advisory groups, clubs.
To create a sense of pride in the school.	Give students important jobs in the school.
To involve students in responsible activity in order to develop their problem-solving skills.	Visit students' and staff homes.
To enhance student understanding of and commitment to decisions, programs, and practices.	Display students' work in classrooms, the office, and hallways.

Table 4 continued page 41

TABLE 4 continued

Objectives	Activities
To have students accept the responsibility for the life within the school.	Widen extracurricular participation; for example, have more students contribute to a school paper or any other project.
To eliminate the "them vs. us" syndrome that divides students and faculty.	Increase the number of extracurricular activities to appeal to more students.
To utilize student resources for improving the school.	Use jackets, T-shirts, buttons, and other symbols to rally school pride.
	Involve students who are hesitant to participate in school activities.
	Emphasize student responsibilities in the school.
	Have students share in keeping the school clean.
	Have beautification projects to give students ownership in the facility.
	Use competitive events such as contests, intramurals, etc., to encourage interest and motivation.
	Appoint faculty "buddies" or advisors to each student to provide personal contact.
	Train staff to interact informally with students.
	Have strong homeroom programs.
	Establish formal student/faculty groups.
	Improve informal student/staff relations.
	Have staff/student social events.

Goal 4. *To develop rules and disciplinary procedures that will promote self-discipline.*

When the general public thinks about school discipline, they think first about rules and the consequences of breaking rules. Yet, poorly developed rules and poor enforcement procedures can actually cause discipline problems. Discipline procedures should be continuously scrutinized to determine whether they are achieving the desired results or whether they are causing some undesirable side effects. The ultimate goal of disciplinary procedures is to teach desirable behavior.

Ideally, rules should be developed with participation from those who are to enforce them and from those who are to obey them. Such participation generates a mutual understanding of what is expected and a personal commitment to abide by the rules. Such participation is as essential to responsible citizenship in a school as it is in a nation; neither can survive for long if enforcement depends solely on outside forces.

Enforcement based upon punishment, while necessary in some cases, is not a productive way to achieve discipline over the long range and is generally ineffective in developing self-discipline. Enforcement is best when staff and students unite to achieve agreed-on goals based on mutual respect and trust.

Another aspect of disciplinary procedures is the provision for due process. Due process is not simply a legal procedure carried out by the courts; it is an essential feature of any system of rule enforcement that assures fair treatment of all parties concerned. Due process is intended to assure the protection of the rule-maker and the system of rules as much as it is intended to protect the individual. The procedures carry out the contract between citizen and state or between the school and its constituents—both students and staff. The school as an institution gives services and protects its members, who in turn give support and loyalty to the institution. The trade-off is mutually beneficial; and when it ceases to be mutually beneficial, one of the parties will break the contract.

Good schools attempt to involve most of their constituents in developing and implementing the rules. Educators in those schools know that those who are not involved in the process will have neither an understanding of the rules nor a commitment to obey them; so they engage in intensive teaching to get both. Not content with merely announcing the rules, they take time to make certain that everyone in the school knows the rules and procedures, understands what is expected, and has some sense of how the rules benefit both the school and the individual.

The following five reports illustrate how schools in our survey developed their disciplinary codes and procedures with the involvement of staff, students, parents and others.

Our discipline code was developed by a committee of parents, teachers, students, and administrators. After the code was developed, workshops were presented to the parents during an evening meeting; and an entire day of school was spent teaching the discipline code to the students. Each member of the committee worked with groups of 25 students answering questions and explaining rules and regulations. A workshop was also provided for the teaching staff and school monitors. An ongoing Review Committee, made up of teachers, students, administrators, and parents, functions to keep the discipline code updated and to make sure that it is being properly implemented. The committee also provides evening workshops for teachers and parents.
—*Roy C. Ketcham High School*
Wappingers Falls, N.Y.

The staff initiated a search to find what was being said by other school boards and high schools concerning discipline policies and procedures. A discipline policy was then drafted, which was reviewed by the high school student council, the citizens' advisory council, the district administrative team, and the board of education. The entire school community and general community was consulted before a plan was developed. High school staff members were instrumental in making recommendations for the plan and were used as chief consultants. They key to success was careful study of other schools.
—*Lena-Winslow High School*
Lena, Ill.

Our school has established Project Involve, which consists of a series of six student commitments with corresponding parent and/or teacher obligations. Students agree to bring study materials to class, raise semester grades, complete a self-evaluation of progress every two weeks, and follow the school's guidelines for behavior. Parents support the students by agreeing to set aside quiet study time, while teachers agree to notify parents of the student's progress. Students who enroll receive a "West Junior Involved" pin. One student is recognized as "Student of the Month" and receives a certificate.
—*West Junior High School*
Colorado Springs, Colo.

Teachers identify students who appear to be having problems and refer them to a staff team, who then make recommendations for placing them in the Prevention Room for part of the day (10% to 50%). The Prevention Room is a highly structured situation with a strong academic orientation and with one-on-one tutoring. The program offers counseling and the teachers report on a daily basis on progress being made. It serves as a time-out placement and early referral to avoid students being sent to the office.
— *Greenfield Junior High School*
Greenfield, Mass.

Our staff has initiated a Saturday Study Session as an alternative to suspensions. School officials report that during the last four years, the suspension rate has been reduced to fewer than 90 a year.
— *Butler High School*
Vandalia, Ohio

Schools in the survey reported many ways of creating a positive atmosphere in the school by recognizing student achievement. Examples included sending "Happy Grams" home, recognizing individuals or groups of students for special achievements, and giving special privileges to students for exhibiting desired behaviors. Many schools also reported ways for students to experience success. Examples from five schools follow.

Four years ago we instituted a program called "target four," which sought to 1) improve communication with the home; 2) increase student enjoyment; 3) improve achievement in the subject skills area; and 4) increase reading skill. Some activities for achieving these goals included improved communication through bulletins and newspapers, information sessions for parents, students representing the school in the community, student crafts exhibits from home, selection of a "student of the month," and awarding "Panther Pride" wallet cards for exceptional recognition. These cards can be used by students for free shows. Also, a "student of the year" award is given by the student council. The program was designed to address the problems of poor school attitudes, low self-image, and low achievement. Staff members report problems were reduced

87% over the four-year period.
>— *Central Elementary School*
> *Roundup, Mont.*

We have attempted to recognize the efforts of all students by instituting a program of commendation letters for those students who have demonstrated a willingness to work hard and learn. The students nominated are not necessarily those who have achieved the highest grades but those who are diligent, progressive workers. Teachers nominate students. A handwritten joint letter from the principal and teacher goes to the parents.
>— *Trinity Middle School*
> *Washington, Pa.*

Our school uses a variety of activities to implement a positive discipline program. The Principal's Award for Leadership (P.A.L.) for citizenship and conduct is given monthly to three students from each homeroom; and these students are featured in the monthly Newsletter that goes to all parents. We use positive reinforcement and behavior contracts to teach self-disciplined behavior. A continuous-progress curriculum keeps each student productively engaged in school work.
>— *Meadows Elementary School*
> *Stafford, Tex.*

This school emphasizes recognizing student achievement. Assemblies are held to honor scholarship winners. Athletes and other students are periodically designated as "someone special" (120 during the year). The school holds breakfasts and posts students' birthdays daily on the bulletin board.
>— *Butler High School*
> *Vandalia, Ohio*

The principal sends home a *Good News Bulletin*, which presents the "good news" of the school and headlines such statistics as: 99% of the students were not suspended or expelled; 97.5% were respectful of staff; 99% were not involved in any vandalism or stealing; 98% were not in a fight or argument; and 25 students gave up recess or lunch to provide service to the school.
>— *Franklin Junior High School*
> *Newark, N.J.*

Table 5 presents some objectives and activities from schools in our survey for developing rules, disciplinary procedures, and a positive school climate. It is important to remember that their discipline programs were integrated into the fabric of the school and were not isolated or separated from academic and extracurricular programs. This integration seemed to be why the disciplinary procedures were working, regardless of the nature of the rules or enforcement procedures.

TABLE 5

OBJECTIVES AND ACTIVITIES FOR DEVELOPING RULES, DISCIPLINARY PROCEDURES, AND A POSITIVE SCHOOL CLIMATE

Goals	Objectives	Activities
A. To Develop Better Rules and Disciplinary Procedures	To insure due process for both staff and students.	Establish clear, reasonable, and enforceable school rules and policies.
	To insure that students understand behavioral expectations of the school.	Involve students and staff in setting up disciplinary procedures.
	To enable teachers to utilize disciplinary procedures consistent with student behavioral needs.	Provide adequate adult supervision in all areas of the schools.
	To give staff the knowledge and skills they need to deal effectively with student behavior problems.	Develop cooperative adult-student plans to enforce school rules.
	To insure that disciplinary actions are congruent with interests of the student.	Develop clearly defined programs for dealing with discipline; e.g., in-school suspensions, "time-out" rooms, peer counseling, student advocates.

Table 5 continued page 47

TABLE 5 continued

Goals	Objectives	Activities
	To insure consistent expectations among staff members.	Involve parents in school discipline.
	To eliminate any organizational causes for discipline problems.	Reward positive student behavior.
		Assess the causes of student behavior problems.
		Use alternatives for traditional discipline methods.
		Use alternative organization patterns to meet student and staff needs.
		Insure school security for persons and property.
		Train staff to use various disciplinary techniques.
B. To Develop a Positive Climate	To give students recognition when they exhibit positive behavior.	Give individual students written communications for positive behavior and accomplishments.
	To foster student motivation to engage in appropriate actions.	Praise students for positive behavior and accomplishments.
	To help staff and students become more aware of the positive things students do.	Use the school intercom to recognize students for contributions to the school.

Table 5 continued page 48

TABLE 5 continued

Goals	Objectives	Activities
	To foster positive interactions among students and adults in the school.	Give special privileges and rewards to students for desired behaviors, e.g., tokens, movies.
	To develop a deeper sense of belonging and loyalty.	Give awards to individual students, e.g., certificates, prizes.
		Create for more students a chance to experience success.
		Have students and teachers work together on projects and share recognition.
		Train staff to recognize and reward good behavior.

Goal 5. *To improve curriculum and instructional practices in order to reach more students.*

Curriculum and instruction are the central business of the schools. Students come to school to learn. If time is not spent learning, there seems little reason to be in school; therefore, students are likely to drop out or to protest the system, because they are not doing what they came there to do. Such protests often appear as discipline problems, because students feel they are not served by the system and cannot tolerate the insecurity that arises when the system is not doing what they expected it to do.

The curriculum establishes the goals a school attempts to achieve. If those goals seem worthwhile and attainable, both staff and students will be committed to achieving them. But if they seem abstract, useless, or unattainable, the staff will have to exert a great deal more energy to persuade students to pursue the curriculum goals. Under such circumstances, the curriculum can actually become a cause of discipline problems. Staff and students are likely to lose interest and settle into a dull routine just to satisfy some outside authority. Neither will take responsibility for making things work.

Similarly, if instructional practices are not related to curriculum goals or do not take into account what students already know and need to know in order to participate, some students will become alienated from classroom activity and proceed to seek other, perhaps disruptive, ways to gain attention or to feel successful. Discipline problems are bound to result if:

- The curriculum goals are not shared and reinforced.
- The curriculum is pursued without students really learning.
- The curriculum provides no choices that recognize staff and student individual styles.
- The curriculum does not relate to anything students or their families have experienced and value.
- The curriculum content has no solid substance.
- Staff are not expected to teach every student.
- Instruction does not begin at the student's level of ability.
- No one cares enough about what the student does to give constructive feedback.
- The student cannot do the work, and no one helps.
- The student continually experiences failure or has a long history of failure in similar activities.
- Instructional methods are consistently dull and uninspiring.
- Staff feel the student cannot learn and the system provides excuses for failure to teach.

Well-disciplined schools have staff who find ways to teach all of their students. The staff believes in the curriculum and the methods of instruction and is committed to making them work; yet, they know that methods must be adapted for different learners.

Activities to enhance curriculum and instruction were often reported by schools in our survey. Many schools emphasized high standards and concentrated on providing a variety of learning activities for students. Communication with parents about academic matters was seen as a deterrent to discipline problems. Special programs enriched the learning atmosphere in many schools. Some examples follow.

Project TREE (Teaching Respect through Environmental Education) is an example of a schoolwide curriculum project that also helps to develop attitudes of self-discipline. The project, designed to develop an awareness of the interrelatedness of all living things, combined a schoolwide multidisciplinary approach to environmental education with the philosophy of William Glasser's *Schools Without Failure*. Students and teachers worked together in problem-solving activities that required a great deal of personal responsibility. The project provided inservice education for staff; an opportunity for student participation in decision making; and an opportunity for students, parents, and other community members to work together toward a common purpose. From September 1975 to September 1976, the school had a 65% decrease in the number of incidents of misbehavior reported to the principal. Since then, inservice efforts and projects have continued in the school.

—Brookside Elementary School
Waterville, Me.

Most of our students are from families in which both parents work. School is the focus of their activities and they often spend time on the playground before and after school. The staff identified a need to teach the students how to make better use of the playgrounds for street hockey, kickball, four square, etc., and taught students how to play. The games were started at one grade level and gradually were extended to all grade levels. Participation in the games was used as a reward for completion of work and for appropriate behavior. The staff found that "troublemakers" became active participants in the tournaments.

—Reeds Ferry Elementary School
Merrimack, N.H.

A strong music program is the heart of our program. Over a third of the students participate in either band or chorus. A championship band and a boy's chorus perform regularly in the community. The administration emphasizes high academic standards. There is an active National Junior Honor Society. A Student Nobel Prize program honors excellence. Parents go back to school one day a year, with 40% attending seminars on curriculum and instruction given by department heads.

—Kennedy Junior High School
Waltham, Mass.

Our school is a pilot school in the Arts in the Basic Curriculum Program. The arts (dance, music, drama, and visual arts) are important to our instructional program. Classroom teachers and specialists receive inservice training in how to include art activities in all parts of the curriculum. Students are enthusiastic about band and string orchestra. Reading is stressed in a voluntary One Hundred Book Club. Outside speakers are brought in to reinforce interest in learning.

—*Diggs Elementary School*
Winston-Salem, N.C.

Table 6 shows objectives and activities that create a curriculum that contributes to the development of a sense of belongingness, satisfaction, and commitment, which are essential for self-disciplined behavior.

TABLE 6

OBJECTIVES AND ACTIVITIES FOR IMPROVING CURRICULUM AND INSTRUCTIONAL PRACTICES TO REMOVE ACADEMIC CAUSES FOR DISCIPLINE PROBLEMS

Objectives	*Activities*
To provide a curriculum that reflects the culture and background of the students served by the school.	Develop a schoolwide curriculum that appeals to a wide range of students interests.
To insure that instructional techniques used by teachers minimize the potential for disruptive behavior.	Develop curriculum to meet specific academic deficiencies, e.g., low reading scores or poor map skills.
To insure that teachers can vary instruction to meet the learning and behavioral needs of students.	Add courses or activities to enrich the curriculum.
To provide students with activities that are interesting and motivating.	Help students with their academic needs; e.g., help with homework, provide quiet place for study, discuss textbook or lecture content.
To provide students with an environment that is conducive to learning.	Tutor students with learning difficulties.
To focus school activities on learning, thereby reducing unproductive activity.	Emphasize high academic standards, but concentrate on basic skills as a foundation for excellence.
	Use a variety of instructional groups to meet staff and student needs.

Table 6 continued on page 52

TABLE 6 continued

Objectives   *Activities*

Train staff to improve curriculum and instruction.

Train staff to obtain resources from the school and from the community.

Systematically evaluate academic progress and resolve problems early.

Goal 6. *To deal with personal problems that affect life within the school.*

Schools are human enterprises; they are made up of people who bring all their strengths and frailties into the school. They worry. They are anxious. They have prejudices. They love and want to be loved. They feel guilty or angry or aggressive. They are shy or dominating. They feel inadequate but think that they shouldn't. They bring all of these feelings onto the job; and if such feelings are sufficiently strong and are not handled well, they can contribute to discipline problems. Arthur Jersild, *When Teachers Face Themselves*, (New York: Teachers College Press, 1955), provides insight into teachers' personal concerns and the effect these concerns have on their behavior.

Good schools find ways to help staff and students deal with their emotions and their personal problems so that life within the school is not adversely affected. Without assuming the role of therapist, staff members can help a colleague or student seek professional help if it seems necessary. A good school can relieve excess pressures and make people feel they have someone to whom they can tell their troubles.

Counseling often reveals the causes of discipline problems; and if the causes reside in school, they can be corrected or removed. The schools in our survey indicated that counseling does not always have to be provided by a designated school counselor. In fact, official counselors are often so busy with scheduling and other duties that there is little time for intensive student/adult counseling, even though they are trained to provide it. Many other avenues for providing counseling were suggested by the survey schools: peer counseling, informal teacher counseling, volunteer professionals, mental health agencies, and many others.

The following three reports from survey schools indicate the extent to which some schools go to provide assistance to staff and students in order to short-circuit the internal feelings that could lead to explosive discipline problems:

> About 15 students are assigned to each instructor in an advisor-advisee program, which is an extension of the guidance department. The advisor-advisee program is particularly helpful at enrollment time because it provides a chance to get to know 15 students on a more personal basis and provides another source of information to parents. The school maintains a communication center that offers group counseling, individual counseling, family counseling, and crisis counseling, which immediately handles incidents of harassment, fighting, theft, vandalism, child abuse, and running away. The crisis counseling often uses rumor control procedures in order to get immediate feedback to concerned staff and students. The trained student-conflict managers and student communicators are used to settle fights so offenders do not need to be suspended. The communication center also provides training for staff members in leading groups, sex education, drugs, human relations, and improving classroom climate. All teachers have attended a workshop on sex equity; and a staff seminar on dealing with stress was substituted for a regular staff meeting.
> —*Independence High School*
> *Independence, Kan.*

Student communicators help to improve the school. Communicators are selected from natural student leaders who are trained to handle conflicts among students. They handle pre-fight arguments, hassles, fight counseling, rumors, personal problems, stealing, threats, and other problems that arise. They are provided two all-day training sessions. They then meet bi-weekly for a period with staff advisors. These students are called out of class when needed to assist in dealing with problems, because they are a credible force when stating consequences to the students in conflict; they are direct and can more easily see the real reasons for a hassle; and they are good problem solvers. Records are kept on incidents. Basically, if the problem is solved and a commitment is made that the problem will not happen again, the administration does not suspend. This program has reduced suspensions considerably.
—*Kerr School*
Elk Grove, Calif.

The Teacher Advocate Program uses teachers on a one-to-one basis to work with students who have special discipline problems. Teachers who volunteer for the program spend extra time with the student both inside and outside the classroom and meet on a weekly basis to discuss their students. They receive special training. The goals of the program are to: 1) give students an advocate who will know them on an academic and a personal basis; 2) help students find help out of school for themselves and their family; 3) enable teachers to understand why discipline problems occur and develop new techniques to deal with them.

—*Ketcham High School*
Wappingers Falls, N.Y.

Table 7 presents objectives and activities that well-disciplined schools reported about their efforts to provide help with personal problems.

TABLE 7
OBJECTIVES AND ACTIVITIES FOR DEALING WITH PERSONAL PROBLEMS

Objectives	*Activities*
To provide help to staff and parents with personal crises.	Provide certified counselors in the schools.
To help school staff identify the causes of misbehavior rather than the symptoms.	Assign staff members as informal counselors to individuals and groups of students.
To provide individual attention for students.	Set up systems for peer counseling.
To provide objective assistance to students and staff.	Secure counseling for students in their homes, in recreation centers, and other areas outside the school.
Provide systematic counseling services for adults, both parents and staff members.	Enlist community agencies, churches, and hospitals to give counseling services to the school.
To provide a way for students and staff to learn to solve their own problems and take responsibility.	Train all staff members to use counseling techniques in their contact with students.
To provide every student a helpful adult contact.	Set up staff programs for financial planning, family counseling for treating alcoholism or other chemical abuse.

Table 7 continued on page 55

TABLE 7 continued

Objectives	Activities
To prevent personal problems from affecting nonrelated school and classroom events.	Foster the development of informal support groups among the faculty and among the students.
To provide healthy outlets for feelings.	Train staff to deal with conflict, frustration, guilt, anger and other human emotions.
	Help staff examine prejudices and their effects on students.
	Eliminate sexist and racist behaviors in school practices and actions.

Goal 7. *To strengthen interaction between the school and the home.*

Much learning takes place beyond the schoolhouse walls. Homes, churches, shopping centers, settlement houses, pool halls, etc. are important places in students' lives. These places and other community resources can be used by a school faculty as part of the curriculum—for field trips, for sources of information, for sources of help—in ways that make the school and community reinforce one another. When students' experiences are limited, community resources outside their immediate neighborhood can expand their horizons.

Schools in our survey identified hundreds of ways for getting into the community. They ranged from what is perhaps the simplest and most effective strategy, making home visits (which was reported by a surprisingly large number of schools), to using radio and television to enhance the school image. Many schools send a variety of written communications to students' homes with a positive message. Some had printed forms with catchy names like "Happy Grams," or "Arrow Grams," which give the school a positive image. In other schools, teachers sent personal notes, or the principal had regular newsletters.

Students also need to know that teachers are interested in them, their families, and the places where they live. Knowing about students' lives in their own communities has important implications for the type of education provided in the school. The school is often isolated, and people in the community often feel little ownership or involvement in what the school is trying to do. Parents, too, often assume that they are unwelcome in the school and may respond to teachers' concerns with indifference or even hostility. Having teachers and other staff members involved in the community is one of the most effective ways to convey that the school cares about the people it serves. Such relationships give parents and students a sense of ownership and a responsibility toward the school.

Many survey schools reported that they involve the community by making wide use of parent/citizen advisory groups. Such groups have real input into school policies and practices. In some cases, such groups even help to hire staff. Most schools reported that school buildings were used by P.T.A. and P.T.O. organizations; and many reported that buildings were used by community groups. Many schools had a large number of volunteers. Parents and citizens came into the school and assisted with instruction or provided enrichment for the program. Several schools reported training programs for parents and volunteers who assisted in the school.

The following excerpts illustrate the variety of school/community interactions reported by the survey schools:

> Our school suffered from a $300,000 fire set by neighborhood young people. In addition there was a tremendous amount of graffiti, broken windows, frequent break-ins, fighting among students, low teacher morale, parent problems, etc. Today the school is beautiful, clean, practically free of graffiti, the result of a plan involving the collaboration of school staff, parents, students, community leaders, central office security staff, and local law-enforcement officers. Some actions — security guards, electronic devices for night security, enlistment of school neighbors, and community education — were instituted to address the symptoms. Causes were more complicated. Caring prevents violence and vandalism far more effectively than an entire arsenal of locks, alarms, etc. So, a major part of the plan was to improve the school climate. The annual Open House attracted 1147 parents this year. That did not happen by accident. Careful planning and activities to make parents feel welcome were part of the project.
>
> —*Franklin School*
> *Newark, N.J.*

> Because of our School Volunteer Program, approximately one-fourth of the students work in the community on a volunteer basis each day.
>
> —*Independence High School*
> *Independence, Kan.*

A public relations committee, composed of two assistant principals, teachers, students, and parents, brainstorms possible projects, selects eight to 10 each year, and assigns specific public relations projects to committee members to complete.
—*Northern Valley Regional High School Demarest, N.J.*

Our high school emphasizes outreach into the community. School activities are advertised, and senior citizens have free admission. The Honor Society has a spaghetti dinner for senior citizens; and the school boasts an active girls' service club called Zonta. Staff members regularly supply programs for community organization meetings. School facilities are used by youth groups, churches, the recreation program, and scouting groups.
—*Pompton Lakes High School Pompton Lakes, N.J.*

Parents are trained to make presentations about the school program to service clubs, other schools in the state, and any interested groups.
—*Central Elementary School Roundup, Mont.*

Table 8 presents objectives and activities for bringing the community into the school and for taking the school into the community.

TABLE 8

OBJECTIVES AND ACTIVITIES THAT STRENGTHEN INTERACTION BETWEEN SCHOOLS AND HOMES AND COMMUNITIES

Goals	Objectives	Activities
A. To Bring the Community into the School	To create community awareness of instructional practices and school policies.	Invite citizens to attend school programs, fairs, open houses, and other events.
	To facilitate greater parent involvement in school activities.	Use the school for meetings—community organizations, adult education, and recreation.

Table 8 continued page 58

TABLE 8 continued

Goals	Objectives	Activities
	To dispel negative feelings toward the school.	Involve citizens and parents in instructional activities.
	To foster the direct involvement of parents with teacher and students in the school milieu.	Involve citizens in decision-making advisory councils, commitees, and conferences.
	To help the community identify with the school.	Involve parents in school disciplinary actions.
	To build a corps of supporters for the school and its staff.	Train parents to assist in the school.
		Use volunteers to provide help in non-instructional roles.
		Seek cooperation between school and community projects.
		Train staff to utilize volunteers.
		Train staff for better parent and community relations.
B. To Take the School into the Community	To give teachers a better understanding of the student's home environment.	Have teachers visit students' homes.
	To enable students to understand that they (and their families) are important to the teacher.	Have teachers make telephone contacts with parents.
	To provide teachers with an opportunity to communicate directly with parents.	Send written communication, such as notes, newsletters, and "Happy Grams" to parents.

Table 8 continued on page 59

TABLE 8 continued

Goals	Objectives	Activities
	To create positive community support for the school's activities and programs.	Use publicity to enhance the school's image.
	To make the school an integral part of community life.	Have staff provide services to the community.
		Use student activities that require greater community involvement.
		Enhance interschool relationships in large school systems.
		Use media to give students visibility in a positive way.
		Have students present programs at community events.
		Have students present radio programs and produce newspapers to be distributed widely.

Goal 8. *To improve the physical facilities and organizational structure of the school to reinforce the other goals.*

Every educator who wants to reduce discipline problems should take a close look at the physical facilities and the way the school is organized. Both the way space is used and the way schedules affect traffic patterns and population density affect the way people work together. Though educators sometimes act as though standardized organization procedures cannot be changed, well-disciplined schools reported numerous departures from standard operating procedures as ways to get better results.

The following excerpts from survey schools illustrate how they used facilities, space, and time to enhance their programs:

The public address system is not used and bells are not rung during school hours. Classes are two hours and 15 minutes in length so students are given time to accomplish their performance objectives. They may take a brief 10-minute nutrition break as needed during the class session.
>—*Denver Career Education Center*
>*Denver, Colo.*

Parents, community leaders, teachers, administrators, and students worked for several weekends to paint the entire outside of the school. The new physical appearance gave visible evidence of caring about the school. Over the door was painted the motto, "We're So Proud."
>—*Franklin School*
>*Newark, N.J.*

Our school sponsors an annual beautification project under the direction of the Student Council.
>—*Stickney Elementary School*
>*Toledo, Ohio*

Staff members state that they don't feel that it takes a special "system" or lots of money to make a good school. The school is full of colors, plants, laughter, and happy people. As much as possible, the goal of the school is to approximate the atmosphere of a loving home. Children are aides. Each unit has kindergarten through third-grade children.
>—*Little Chute Elementary School*
>*Little Chute, Wisc.*

Table 9 shows objectives and activities that improve facilities and organization in ways that support efforts to improve school discipline.

TABLE 9

OBJECTIVES AND ACTIVITIES THAT IMPROVE PHYSICAL FACILITIES AND ORGANIZATIONAL STRUCTURES THAT AFFECT SCHOOL DISCIPLINE

Objectives	*Activities*
To use the physical setting to teach students what the school stands for and is.	Have "painting projects" and other school decoration or beautification projects.
To increase a sense of student belongingness.	Display student work in the school.
To discourage vandalism and graffiti.	Establish "cafeteria committees" of students and teachers to make the eating place more like a restaurant and less institutional.
To give students visible evidence that the school serves and cares about them.	Stagger schedules to improve traffic patterns in the school.
To increase positive attitudes on the part of the staff, students, and parents.	Adjust schedules to permit large and small group instruction.
To provide pleasant surroundings in which people can work.	Provide decorations and displays that reflect students' homes and backgrounds.
To use facilities and schedules to support the school program.	Ask community agencies, businesses, and individuals to help create more attractive physical facilities.
	Keep the school in good repair and maintenance.
	Train staff to make creative use of space and time.
	Include custodial staff in faculty meetings.
	Cluster units in a large school to make smaller, more personal "community" groupings.
	Mix grade levels or subject matter teachers as often as possible to reduce divisions among staff and students.

Using this Chapter for School Improvement

All schools have resources that can be used for needed improvement. This chapter has shown how well-disciplined schools found ways to mobilize and organize their resources to improve school operations that affect school discipline, achievement, morale, and public confidence. Their reports indicate that much can be done to change established school practices; and their experience can inspire any school staff to tackle problems that seem unsolvable.

This chapter is a stimulus for ideas. A school staff or parent group may wish to read the whole chapter or to review the tables of activities to get ideas. Then, groups can be formed to identify local problems, to generate activities, and to make improvements using the procedures discussed in the chapters that follow.

4

The Discipline Context Inventory: A Stimulus for Positive Faculty Action

School staff often need some way to sort out which problems are most important and should be dealt with first. The *Inventory* presented in this chapter is designed to help school staff think about a broad range of school characteristics that influence discipline either positively or negatively. Once these characteristics are identified and analyzed, the staff can then decide on which of the most serious problems to work. At the end of this chapter, we outline a series of steps for using the *Inventory* in staff meetings devoted to improving self-discipline in the school.

How is the Inventory Related to Discipline?

Discipline is learned. Behavior is caused. Those two sentences should be engraved on the wall of every teachers' lounge, every administrator's office, and every college teacher-education classroom. When students misbehave, the misbehavior is caused. To attempt to end the misbehavior, one must first find the cause. If we want students to behave appropriately, we must find ways for them to learn new behavior.

The *Inventory* evolved from a search for causes of desired and undesired behavior in schools. The search soon showed that staff in well-disciplined schools create conditions and use practices that cause students to accept responsibility and to behave appropriately, even when no one is there to make them do it. In other words, these staffs know that many common practices in schools are the cause for much misbehavior, but they have consciously modified the climate in their schools in order to teach good discipline.

The idea that the school itself may be the cause of discipline problems makes some people angry; they are impatient with those who blame the schools for all the world's problems. But no one has to be blamed. A driver is not to blame if the car stops because of a flat tire. But the driver may be faulted if he stands around complaining "It isn't my fault" rather than getting the tire replaced or repaired. Similarly, if the school schedule is causing problems, there is nothing to be gained by blaming someone. What is important is to get the schedule reorganized so the school can run more effectively. If a student cannot hear what the teacher is saying, the student is likely to become restless. If this happens day after day, the student mentally drops out and may become disruptive. The sensible thing to do is to find a way for the student to hear and participate, such as having the teacher talk louder, providing a microphone for the teacher, or simply moving the student nearer the teacher. Another example is school policy on extracurricular activities that may prevent a student from participating. When such a policy causes a student to be left out of important and rewarding activities, that student may lose interest in school and become a "discipline problem." The solution is to revise the policy. Everyone can probably remember school practices or policies that caused frustration or resentment and led to disruptive or withdrawn behavior.

The *Inventory* identifies eight factors in school life that have a powerful influence on student (and staff) behavior. The commission's study of schools with good discipline showed that those schools were using these same eight factors to teach good behavior. They are:

• the way people work together to solve problems or to make decisions about how the school operates;
  • the way authority and status are distributed in the school;
  • the degree to which students feel they belong in the school;
  • the way rules are stated, understood, and enforced;
  • the formal curriculum and the style of instruction;
  • the way in which personal problems are handled;
  • relationships with parents and the surrounding community; and
  • the appearance, organization, and utilization of the building and the grounds.

These eight factors make up the living curriculum of the school; they convey to everyone in the school "how we behave around here." They show how an individual fits into the school every minute of the day, how he or she will be rewarded, and how to behave to receive those rewards. Improving discipline in a school can best be achieved by examining these eight factors and by taking action to make them cause the behavior desired.

The Discipline Context Inventory*

Introduction: This inventory is neither a "score card" nor an objective test. It is a working guide for use by school personnel, students, and parents to analyze programs and to identify problem areas on which they wish to work to reduce disruption and to improve discipline in their schools.

Directions: Circle a number to rate your school on a scale of 0 to 5 with a rating of 0 indicating that the statement is not at all true of your school and a rating of 5 indicating that the statement is clearly true of your school.

1. *The way people work together for problem solving and decision making.* Generally, more open and widespread participation is related to fewer disruptive behaviors and greater feelings of responsibility among teachers and students.

1.1	0 1 2 3 4 5	Faculty meetings are for staff development and problem solving.
1.2	0 1 2 3 4 5	Faculty members communicate concerns about district policies to central administration and modify those policies for their students' benefit.
1.3	0 1 2 3 4 5	A sense of direction and mutual purpose is shared among a significant number of staff, students, and, to some extent, parents. They can describe goals and achievements in specific, understandable terms.

---

*Copyright ©1977 William W. Wayson. Revision copyright 1979. Permission granted to Phi Delta Kappa to reprint in *Handbook for Developing Schools With Good Discipline*. Any school that wishes to reproduce this *Inventory* for use in local staff development programs is granted permission to do so.

1.4   0 1 2 3 4 5   The school district central administration expects problems to be solved by local staff and community.

1.5   0 1 2 3 4 5   Problems do not fester; they are identified and resolved. The attitude, "What can we do?" replaces the attitude, "It can't be done."

1.6   0 1 2 3 4 5   The school district provides time and consultants to aid in solving problems.

1.7   0 1 2 3 4 5   Adults in the school recognize their own responsibilities for handling situations or for solving problems that affect themselves or the students.

1.8   0 1 2 3 4 5   A large number of the staff are involved in planning and in implementing school activities. Participation is high and widely distributed.

1.9   0 1 2 3 4 5   Staff and students feel that the school belongs to them and that they can make a difference in it.

1.10   0 1 2 3 4 5   Staff exhibit a sense of accomplishment, giving a positive tone to the climate of the school.

1.11   0 1 2 3 4 5   Staff recognize their own problems and don't take them out on the students.

1.12   0 1 2 3 4 5   Staff communicate openly and frequently with one another about significant educational matters.

1.13   0 1 2 3 4 5   Staff are relaxed and not afraid of their students.

1.14   0 1 2 3 4 5   Staff know how to prevent discipline problems caused by adults, by school procedures, or by the school organization.

2. *The distribution of authority and status.* Generally, when there are fewer barriers to communication, more involvement in exercising authority, and fewer status differences, the result is a more widespread sense of responsibility and a greater commitment among staff and students.

2.1	0 1 2 3 4 5	Status differences among various staff groups are eliminated.
2.2	0 1 2 3 4 5	No one ignores problems, refuses to do what needs to be done, or says "It's not my job."
2.3	0 1 2 3 4 5	Administrators' expectations are clearly communicated.
2.4	0 1 2 3 4 5	Staff members generally agree on what principals, teachers, aides, etc., are expected to do in given circumstances.
2.5	0 1 2 3 4 5	Teachers are able to communicate concerns, questions, or constructive ideas to "superiors."
2.6	0 1 2 3 4 5	Each person accepts criticism from those who receive his/her services.
2.7	0 1 2 3 4 5	School secretaries, aides, custodians, bus drivers, and other school staff participate in faculty meetings and inservice sessions.
2.8	0 1 2 3 4 5	Parents participate in classrooms and school activities and are represented in most faculty meetings and inservice sessions.
2.9	0 1 2 3 4 5	Teachers help one another solve problems rather than criticize other teachers or students.
2.10	0 1 2 3 4 5	Responsibilities and "territories" are shared and respected; people are not possessive nor are they fearful that someone will "take over" their job, space, or materials. They say "our school" and "our students" not "mine."
2.11	0 1 2 3 4 5	Status differences among student groups that segregate or limit communications are eliminated.

3. *Student belongingness.* Students feel that the school serves their needs, is a safe and happy place to be, treats them as valued individuals, and provides ways in which student concerns are treated fairly. When students feel supported and are involved in the life of the school, fewer disruptions or irresponsible behaviors will occur.

3.1	0 1 2 3 4 5	Students participate in solving the problems of the classroom and the school.

3.2	0 1 2 3 4 5	A large number of the students are involved in planning and implementing the school's activities. Students feel that the school belongs to them and that they can make a difference in it.
3.3	0 1 2 3 4 5	Students exhibit a sense of accomplishment, giving a positive tone to the climate of the school.
3.4	0 1 2 3 4 5	Teachers know the names of their students, not only those in their classrooms but others in the school.
3.5	0 1 2 3 4 5	Students take responsibility for enforcing the agreed-on rules and procedures with their peers and with teachers and administrators.
3.6	0 1 2 3 4 5	When making school policy decisions, the educational growth of students takes priority over concerns such as adult convenience, pleasing superiors, saving face, or maintaining tradition.
3.7	0 1 2 3 4 5	Students take responsibility for their actions.
3.8	0 1 2 3 4 5	Students are included as members of the school.
3.9	0 1 2 3 4 5	Students' work is displayed in classrooms, display cases, corridors, and cafeterias.
3.10	0 1 2 3 4 5	Students are involved in planning school decorations.
3.11	0 1 2 3 4 5	Students feel responsible for keeping the school environment attractive and clean.
3.12	0 1 2 3 4 5	Students may use the facilities freely as long as there is consideration for other students and for adults.
3.13	0 1 2 3 4 5	When necessary, basic needs of students from poor families are met through whatever resources are available without "spot-lighting" them.
3.14	0 1 2 3 4 5	Children with special problems are diagnosed and help is provided in a manner that does not stigmatize them or separate them from normal school activities.
3.15	0 1 2 3 4 5	Teachers respect the students' language and culture.

3.16	0 1 2 3 4 5	Each student has at least one contact on the faculty, who serves as an advocate.
3.17	0 1 2 3 4 5	Students believe the school offers what they need and find school interesting.
3.18	0 1 2 3 4 5	All students are included in all classroom and school activities, regardless of sex, race, religion, socio-economic status, or academic ability.

4. *Procedures for developing and implementing rules.* Generally, when rules are made by the people involved and when expectations are clearly understood, there are fewer transgressions. The more nearly rules are derived from principles of learning and of normal human behavior, the more effective they are. The more the school operates like a community, as opposed to a prison or army, the fewer the problems.

4.1	0 1 2 3 4 5	Rules and expectations are clearly defined, stated, and communicated so that people know what to do.
4.2	0 1 2 3 4 5	Students are involved in rule making.
4.3	0 1 2 3 4 5	Rules are made by the people who must enforce them.
4.4	0 1 2 3 4 5	Disciplinary techniques are used to teach positive ways of behaving, not to punish or to teach blind obedience.
4.5	0 1 2 3 4 5	A few good rules are made and enforced rather than having too many rules that are not enforced.
4.6	0 1 2 3 4 5	Rules are enforced in a way that will reinforce the behavior that is desired.
4.7	0 1 2 3 4 5	Unenforceable rules are eliminated.
4.8	0 1 2 3 4 5	Due process is applied before punishment.
4.9	0 1 2 3 4 5	Students and others are assumed to be innocent until proven guilty of infractions.
4.10	0 1 2 3 4 5	A complete description of what transpired during any discipline incident is expected from adults and students.
4.11	0 1 2 3 4 5	Teachers are not assumed to be "right" all the time.

4.12 0 1 2 3 4 5   Students are not punished if such punishment has no positive educational outcome.

4.13 0 1 2 3 4 5   Rules and disciplinary procedures are examined and revised to prevent negative educational outcomes such as lower self-respect, dislike for school, lack of responsibility for one's own behavior, sense of helplessness, etc.

4.14 0 1 2 3 4 5   Rules apply only to behavior that has a direct effect on the school or classroom, not to matters that are trivial or highly personal.

5. *Curriculum and instructional practices.* A curriculum that emphasizes learning that is appropriate for the students served and that provides a greater variety of materials and activities tends to reduce discipline problems.

5.1 0 1 2 3 4 5   The curriculum is viewed as more than the content to be taught in subject matter classes.

5.2 0 1 2 3 4 5   Administrative procedures are related to the explicit curriculum goals of the school.

5.3 0 1 2 3 4 5   Field trips, outside speakers, and other good practices are seen as ordinary teaching methods that teachers may utilize without excessive administrative procedures.

5.4 0 1 2 3 4 5   A variety of teaching styles is evident among faculty members.

5.5 0 1 2 3 4 5   Individual differences and differences in learning styles are respected and accommodated.

5.6 0 1 2 3 4 5   Students may transfer from one teacher to another, or one program to another, depending upon their learning styles and their particular educational goals.

5.7 0 1 2 3 4 5   Teachers choose the methods and materials that serve best for achieving their goals.

5.8 0 1 2 3 4 5   Teaching methods and instructional materials build on what the student already knows.

5.9 0 1 2 3 4 5   Students have choices in schedules and assignments.

5.10	0 1 2 3 4 5	The curriculum includes teaching students how to make choices.
5.11	0 1 2 3 4 5	Teaching methods provide for active learning and are neither boring nor frustrating.
5.12	0 1 2 3 4 5	Counterproductive practices are changed or eliminated as speedily as alternatives can be developed.
5.13	0 1 2 3 4 5	The student/teacher ratio is reasonably low.
5.14	0 1 2 3 4 5	Playgrounds, school buses, cafeterias, and hallways, are viewed as places where students learn; teachers design and implement curriculum for those areas.
5.15	0 1 2 3 4 5	Students are frequently involved in learning activities outside the classroom and in the community.
5.16	0 1 2 3 4 5	Some failure is accepted as a natural part of learning and growth.

6. *Processes for dealing with personal problems.* Generally, practices that help people cope with their lives outside the school and with problems that are not directly related to school matters stimulate greater commitment to participate fully in the work of the school.

6.1	0 1 2 3 4 5	Before rushing to solve a problem, people clarify whether there is a problem and define what it is.
6.2	0 1 2 3 4 5	Individual and cultural differences are respected and valued and are allowed to be openly expressed in the school.
6.3	0 1 2 3 4 5	Staff and students recognize that even "good" students and "good" teachers have problems.
6.4	0 1 2 3 4 5	Students are permitted to have "low days."
6.5	0 1 2 3 4 5	Teachers are permitted to feel angry, to have "low days," or to make mistakes.
6.6	0 1 2 3 4 5	Staff understand student behavior and avoid causing problems when there are none.
6.7	0 1 2 3 4 5	Students do not try to manipulate adults.

6.8	0 1 2 3 4 5	Minor student misbehavior does not warrant undue attention.
6.9	0 1 2 3 4 5	Teachers are able to discern when a discipline incident is over.
6.10	0 1 2 3 4 5	Staff do not get distracted from what they want the students to do.
6.11	0 1 2 3 4 5	Teachers do not escalate small problems into larger ones.
6.12	0 1 2 3 4 5	Staff and students express and discuss problems as they arise rather than tucking them away.
6.13	0 1 2 3 4 5	If a person has a problem with another, he or she discusses it *directly* with that person.
6.14	0 1 2 3 4 5	When dissatisfied with their own performance, people focus on growing and do not punish themselves for being short of perfection.
6.15	0 1 2 3 4 5	Both students and staff can give tangible examples of growth that has occurred in adults or students.
6.16	0 1 2 3 4 5	All people in the school recognize and celebrate (even in small ways) when one of them achieves something good.
6.17	0 1 2 3 4 5	People help one another in ways that help them to become independent.
6.18	0 1 2 3 4 5	Teachers and students admit feelings that are causing them to behave inappropriately, but do not blame others for their own feelings.

7. *Relationships with parents and other community members.* Generally, more open relationships with parents and other community members result in better achievement and behavior in the school. Close home and community contacts also enhance the students' sense of belonging.

7.1	0 1 2 3 4 5	Teachers and administrators frequently participate in groups and organizations within the community that can offer support to students and to the school.
7.2	0 1 2 3 4 5	Teachers know the students' parents, homes, and community and frequently interact with them.

7.3	0 1 2 3 4 5	Teachers know the neighborhood, the street names, the stores, and the places of entertainment of their students.
7.4	0 1 2 3 4 5	Teachers recognize they may hold stereotypes about some students and parents as individuals and try in various ways to break down their stereotypes.
7.5	0 1 2 3 4 5	Teachers and other school personnel visit students' homes frequently.
7.6	0 1 2 3 4 5	Each teacher visits the home of every homeroom student (or advisee) early in the school year before any problem can arise.

8. *Physical environment.* Generally, environments that are pleasant for adults and students to work in and that reflect the interests, culture, and values of students encourage good behavior. The more the school environment looks like a workshop, a library, a restaurant, or a conference center and less like a prison or institution, the fewer the problems.

8.1	0 1 2 3 4 5	Meeting and social areas are not crowded.
8.2	0 1 2 3 4 5	Adequate materials are available and they are organized for easy access and clean-up.
8.3	0 1 2 3 4 5	The physical environment is well organized in order to permit a maximum of student independence and behavior.
8.4	0 1 2 3 4 5	Necessary space and adequate facilities are available for student work.
8.5	0 1 2 3 4 5	The school plant is well-planned to accommodate easy movement within and between classrooms and large group areas.
8.6	0 1 2 3 4 5	The cafeteria has places where small groups can sit, eat, and talk quietly together.
8.7	0 1 2 3 4 5	There are several "nooks and crannies" where individuals may be alone to think, read, or work.
8.8	0 1 2 3 4 5	Places are designed where small groups can work together without having to talk loudly to be heard.

8.9   0 1 2 3 4 5   The school is attractive and inviting.

8.10   0 1 2 3 4 5   Staff feel responsible for keeping the school environment attractive and clean.

8.11   0 1 2 3 4 5   Staff and students are able to analyze "trouble areas" in the environment and make provision to solve problems.

8.12   0 1 2 3 4 5   The environment is well-designed acoustically.

8.13   0 1 2 3 4 5   Traffic patterns are analyzed to eliminate causes of discipline problems.

Using the Inventory for Problem-Solving Meetings

The *Inventory* may be used with faculty or parent groups to identify problems in the school and to establish goals for solving those problems. The following procedure is suggested, but adaptations may be made to suit local conditions.

Step 1. Begin by selecting only one of the eight sections in the *Inventory* for rating your school. The selection may be made by asking the faculty to rank the eight areas to determine which one they would be most interested in working on or which one needs most attention in the school. Or the principal or other party could decide which one needs most attention. Sometimes a recent incident in the school might determine on which one to focus.

Step 2. Involve staff early in the process prior to the faculty meeting. Through informal conversations with staff, present the ideas in the *Inventory* and get their suggestions about which ones need attention. Distribute an open-ended questionnaire soliciting the staff's ideas about the major causes of discipline problems (or other problems) in the school. Distribute evidence of problems such as achievement test results, or suspension rates, or incidence of some disruptive behavior, then use the *Inventory* as suggested to get at the causes.

Step 3. Use only one of the eight sections of the *Inventory* for the content of a staff meeting. Staff meetings are too short to deal with the entire range of items included in the *Inventory*. The staff might be overwhelmed or become frustrated if presented with too many items.

Step 4. Divide the staff into groups of five, consisting of members from different departments, different status levels (include noncertified personnel), different grade levels, different sexes, and different races. Have them seat themselves in circles so as to facilitate direct eye contact and discussion.

Step 5. Give each group sheets of chart paper, a marker, and some masking tape for hanging the charts on the wall.

Step 6. Have each person rate the school on all of the items in the section that has been selected for the meeting. The rating can be done before the meeting starts, at the beginning of the meeting, or just after the small groups have been assigned in Step 4. The rating should be done individually and with no discussion among the group.

Step 7. Ask the staff to read the introduction to the *Inventory* so they will understand why they are doing the next steps. Encourage the staff to discuss the introduction to clarify their thinking or to voice their disagreements. Try to get all staff to participate and avoid letting one person act as the "expert" on the *Inventory* and the rationale behind it.

Step 8. Have each group discuss their ratings; then list on the chart the three or four items that have the highest ratings and the three or four that have the lowest ratings in their group.

Step 9. Have the whole staff look at the charts showing the strongest and weakest items for the school; then the whole group should develop a list of the items that most need attention. Items for the list should be selected through consensus, not through voting. Consensus requires that all disagreements are stated, heard, and considered, and that all participants agree before final action is taken. Voting divides groups into "winners" and "losers" and reduces feelings of responsibility for carrying out the decision. For more on consensus, consult "Techniques to Facilitate Consensus," in R. A. Schmuck, and P.J. Runkel, *Handbook of Organization Development in Schools.* (Eugene, Oregon: University of Oregon, Center for Advanced Study of Educational Administration, 1972), pp. 259-60; or *Second Handbook of Organization Development in Schools.* (Palo Alto, Calif.: Mayfield Publishing, 1977), pp. 323-325, 344-352.

Step 10. Using the list developed by the whole group (Step 9), have each individual categorize the items by using the following questions:

1. Which items do you think you cannot do anything about?
2. Which items do you not want to do anything about?
3. Which items do you think you could do something about and want to do something about?

Step 11. Use the answers to question 3 above to assign committees to work on one item with the intention of improving it. Have each committee submit a work plan at the next faculty meeting showing what will be done, by whom, and on what timeline? Use the problem-solving and planning procedures suggested in Chapter 5, Fig. 2. on page 93.

Step 12. Have each group report progress at each faculty meeting. Provide suggestions and help as indicated. Discuss progress informally between meetings.

5
How Can A School Get Started on Improvement?

Most teachers and administrators have had little formal training in ways to go about changing and improving their schools. Problem solving and program development are not easy to carry out. Such techniques often have to be learned through experience or taught as part of inservice education. But no problem need go unattended because there are no trained planners on the staff. The techniques can be learned by most people who want to learn them. The purpose of this chapter, then, is to present the steps involved in successful school change, to provide a few basic planning techniques, and to encourage more people to participate in school improvement.

We have to confess a bias here. We do not believe that cosmetic changes are worth the time and effort required to install them. Effective school improvements require meticulous attention to bringing the organization along to a new level of operation that will truly resolve problems without incurring undesirable side effects. School improvement, as we envision it, is a process for addressing real problems with the sincere intention of resolving them. The changes that we envision (which we feel characterize the schools in our survey) are not "whipped cream on mud" or publicity stunts but rather are designed to make better educational programs with real and long-lasting positive effects.

Some Principles to Guide School Improvement

There are a number of myths about the change process as it relates to school improvements. A few basic principles may help to counteract some of these myths. Although the following principles may not be a revelation to some readers, many teachers, administrators, and other staff members have found them helpful for understanding the dynamics of change.

Principle 1. The change process is not as rational as planners would lead us to believe. Nearly all systems for planning and decision making are designed as though the world is rational and as though all possibilities can be anticipated and accounted for. Wrong. Anyone who works with schools (or with any other human enterprise) for very long knows that people in organizations often behave quite irrationally; organizations themselves have their own irrationalities.

Being right is not enough to make a change happen. There may be many different "right" ways to view a problem or to resolve it. But even if you think you have the only right assessment and the only right answer, the organization may not welcome the news. One should not expect that having correct information and proven solutions will make everyone do what is supposed to be done. People in organizations just simply do not respond to information that way. They may deny the information or criticize the solution; they may denounce the person who proposes the change.

Principle 2. Someone benefits from preserving the status quo, no matter how bad or non-productive it seems to be. No matter how bad a situation may be, someone benefits by having it stay as it is. For example, faculty members in schools that have had poor discipline for a long time find time-honored excuses for doing nothing to improve the discipline, to improve their teaching, or to establish contacts with parents. They may feel that nothing can be done and are quick to come up with reasons why nothing will work. Schools that have little or no contact with parents and little interaction with the community often have faculty members whose out-of-school life precludes ever having such contact. In school they feel that parent contact is an imposition upon their workday. Because they are satisfied with the status quo, they may resist any change. Consciously or unconsciously, they will obstruct any effort to increase contact with parents, even though more contact may improve school discipline, staff morale and productivity, and community regard for teachers.

Any attempt to change these persons will lead to clashes, the outcome of which will determine whether the school will improve or will remain mediocre or worse.

Principle 3. Not everyone has to be involved in order to bring about improvement. Fortunately, successful change does not seem to depend upon having everyone in the school eager to make the change. As few as one-third of the staff can make changes, especially when their efforts show results that attract others to get on the bandwagon. When the principal is part of that one-third, the chances of success are increased markedly.

Principle 4. Successful change depends not only on thorough planning but also upon the ability to take advantage of unexpected occurrences. Although planning is important, serendipity (taking advantage of unexpected incidents that open up new opportunities) accounts for many successes. A death or retirement of a faculty member, or a natural disaster such as a school fire, or adding a new assistant principal can trigger a change. Those who wish to improve their schools must be able to take advantage of serendipitous events when they occur.

Principle 5. Someone must feel the need to improve and must have the will and perseverance to make it happen. Someone must recognize a problem. While not all school improvements are planned, most of those we found in the survey schools occurred because someone in the school or community felt a need to make a change, to make something better than it was. Someone must have the desire and willingness to do the hard work that is necessary to carry the reform through to completion.

While will and enthusiasm alone are not enough to bring about improvements, they can go a long way in overcoming other planning and organizing deficiencies.

Principle 6. If you think improvement is impossible, it will be. Do not let the attitude of "this won't work" become an obstacle to success. The programs developed and operated in the survey schools illustrated that the principals, staffs, and community members found that obstacles yielded before determined efforts to overcome them. For example, unions and negotiated contracts are frequently cited as reasons why schools cannot change. Yet the staffs in the schools surveyed did far more than many administrators believe teachers will do "in this age of unionism." Many of these schools are in strong union cities, and many of the teachers are loyal members of their local teacher union or association. Nevertheless, they did all sorts of things that it is commonly believed that unions or union thinking might prohibit. They painted schools; they took on extra-class duties; they visited homes; they helped students after school; they organized activities; and they attended all sorts of meetings at all hours of the day and on all days of the week. The point of view that says "They won't do it" is erroneous when one examines the data from our survey schools. Perhaps the most that one can say about improvements in unionized schools is that a different, less authoritarian kind of leadership is required to mobilize professional commitment, zeal, and energy. That may be true of most human enterprises in America at this stage of our history.

Principle 7. Successful change may still be achieved in the worst of situations. Many of the schools surveyed had experienced severe discipline problems previously. They had to overcome faculty apathy, student hostility, community opposition, and personal frustration.

> The students were fighting, cursing, extorting other students, stealing, cutting class, using drugs, and smoking. Many were often rude, defiant; some were withdrawn. They lacked self-esteem and self-direction, had little supervision at home, lacked guidance and attention, had low academic performance, and a deep sense of mistrust.
> —*Mann Opportunity School*
> *North Miami, Fla.*

> Students were disrespectful to staff and each other. Classroom instruction was suffering because of student misbehavior. Absenteeism was high among adult employees, i.e., custodians, staff, food service personnel. The condition of the physical plant was deteriorating due to student vandalism. There was lack of personal and school pride and a high degree of student polarization.
> —*French Junior High School*
> *Lansing, Mich.*

It appears that schools cannot be too bad to change; although it may be they can be too good to change.

Principle 8. Lack of resources is an excuse, not a reason, for doing nothing. Lack of resources is not a reason for failing to improve our schools. Resources alone do not bring change. Schools already have the resources or have access to the resources they need to solve most problems. The problem is to free those resources or to redefine the problem so it can be resolved within the limits of available resources. For example, if a staff feels that it cannot maintain good discipline unless the student/teacher ratio is reduced to 15 to 1, little is likely to happen because fiscal constraints make such a ratio out of the question. However, if the staff faces this reality and then redefines the problem to say, "We cannot do a better job until there are more adults in this school," then the staff can set about to reallocate the time and functions of personnel in the building and to secure volunteers from many sources—parents, retired persons, college students—to enlarge the resource pool.

Steps to Success

Improving school discipline is a process that must take place in *individual school buildings*. The forces that contribute to disruptive behavior evolve from the human interaction among *a* group of school personnel, *a* group of students, in *a* community. Therefore, the following "Steps to Success" are addressed to school personnel, students, and parents in individual schools. Actions taken at districtwide or statewide levels should reinforce and facilitate the local staff's ability to carry out these steps.

Step 1. *Know what goals you want to reach.* The key to successful change requires an enthusiastic and energetic leader and staff with clear goals and specific ideas about how to achieve those goals. Frequently statements of goals are written with no other purpose than to satisfy the requirements of a funding agency or to fulfill some meaningless administrative request. In such cases goals have no personal meaning and are not seen as having any real purpose. If the leader has no clear sense of where the group is going, any change effort is likely to be superficial and short-lived. By asking the question, "What new conditions will exist and what old ones will be eliminated if our goal is achieved?" leaders can be much clearer in their direction.

It is also useful to separate which of the goals are *instrumental* and which are *terminal*. An instrumental goal is one that helps you to get somewhere; the terminal goal is the somewhere you want to get. For example, a school staff may set out to create an in-house suspension program. That is an instrumental goal, not an end in itself. It is the method for creating some new condition in the school in order to eliminate the behaviors for which students are being suspended (the terminal goal). Failure to make such a distinction can lead to the installation of all sorts of instrumental practices that get wrong results or no results. For example, one school felt its high suspension rate (136%) was highly successful because "It gets rid of the kids we don't feel we ought to work with." Achieving instrumental goals that result in indefensible terminal goals is a waste of effort and will not result in better disciplined staff or better disciplined students.

Although you must know what goals you are trying to achieve, every effort must be used to make the goals real for the staff, students and parents. The key is to have staff work on problems that are real for them, that they feel can be resolved, and that they are committed to doing something about. Many schools begin by conducting a needs assessment.

A genuine needs assessment is more than a checklist or open-ended questionnaire given to staff and people in the community. An in-depth needs assessment requires intelligent and insightful analyses that go beyond the perceived needs that the participants in the assessment may have. People may not be aware of what is needed until they know what the alternatives are. Polls and opinion surveys may not bring to light the most crucial factors or problems that must be addressed. Majority votes and average responses are poor measures on which to base change. It is the task of leadership to expand the staff's view of a problem situation by presenting them with new alternatives before they make choices, or by conducting staff development sessions designed to introduce new information and options. Many schools in our survey sent people to visit other schools to see plans in action before beginning a new plan.

Step 2. *Get the people who must implement the change to "own" the change.* Good communication is essential to insure that everyone is clear about goals and procedures. To get the staff to "buy into" an idea is easier if they have already participated in identifying the goals and in working out ways to attain them.

Staff will feel ownership of an idea for improvement if

- they feel that the problem is real for them;
- they feel they helped to identify the problem and to develop the solution;
- they think they can solve it;
- they think it is part of their responsibility to solve it;
- they realize they will "pay the consequences" for not solving it but will "reap the reward" for solving it.

The most effective way to have the participants "buy into" the effort is to have them involved in the planning right from the beginning, recognizing, of course, that ideas usually begin with one or two people, who then enlist others in the effort. Many methods have been developed to help school staffs identify problems and to engage in problem solving. Chapter 4 presents a way for using the *Discipline Context Inventory* to involve staff in identifying factors in their school that can be contributing to poor discipline. Chapter 3 suggests activities for improving self-disciplined behavior among both staff and students.

Eileen Breckinridge (a pseudonym), in "Improving School Climate," *Phi Delta Kappan* (December 1976), describes a problem identification and planning technique called 1-3-6. The technique was used successfully by William Maynard and the staff of Cleveland High School in Seattle. We have also used it in several schools. Any staff can adapt the procedure to their own circumstances. The steps are simple.

1. Have each person write a private list of concerns about the school.

2. With three people in each group, have groups consolidate the individual lists. Each person has the assignment to make sure that all items get on the consolidated list. No one may criticize any entry.

3. Pair two groups of three to make groups of six. Have these larger groups consolidate the lists created in the trio groups and write them on chart paper. (Variation: have them read aloud by each group while someone records on chart paper.)

4. Hang the chart paper around the walls and give each concern an identifying letter. (A to Z).

5. Have each person in the room rank the problems in terms of importance. (Variations: rank in terms of interest or willingness to work on the problem or in terms of its solvability.)

6. Compute the average rank assigned each problem and post the average on the charts. (Note: this process can be speeded by having each participant compute part of the rankings.)

7. Select the top 10 (or some other number) concerns based upon the average ranks assigned.

8. Have individuals volunteer to work on one of the problems that appear in the top rankings.

9. Use some problem-solving strategy to move toward solution and to teach faculty members how to tackle other problems.

Brainstorming is a widely-used technique for generating a number of ideas in a short time without first subjecting those ideas to criticism, which so often reduces participation and kills good ideas before they get a hearing. If the technique has been used too often and with no follow-up, staffs may become cynical about it, or worse, see it as only an exercise that does not lead to any action. Nevertheless, when used at the beginning of planning sessions, it can draw out lots of ideas and generate a lot of participation—both essential for getting staff to feel a part of the improvement process. Again the rules are simple.

1. Be sure the problem to be addressed is clear to all participants.
2. Assign a time limit (usually a few minutes) for the activity.
3. Encourage everyone to participate.
4. Permit no criticism or negative reaction or discussion about any item during the brainstorming.
5. Write suggestions on chart paper as fast as they are generated, using the participant's words.
6. Accept any suggestion.
7. Encourage "hitchhiking" (building on or taking off from another idea).
8. Discuss the list after it is completed to clarify or to amplify the ideas. Permit clarifying questions but no criticism.
9. Establish priorities based upon feasibility and desirability for pursuing the ideas as possible action plans. Now criticism and exchanges of ideas may be useful.

Force-field analysis is a technique used to identify what is working against the solution of a problem and what is working for the solution. By using the technique a staff can decide what they can change and what they cannot; what they want to deal with and what they do not. First, the problem must be clearly understood by the staff. Then, through brainstorming or other techniques, the staff lists specific forces that are pushing the school toward its goals and forces that are pushing away from the goal. Once these forces have been identified and discussed, then the staff can choose which of the forces can be modified, eliminated, or enhanced and set out to take action for changing them. A chart similar to Fig. 1 may be used to record information, which can then be analyzed.

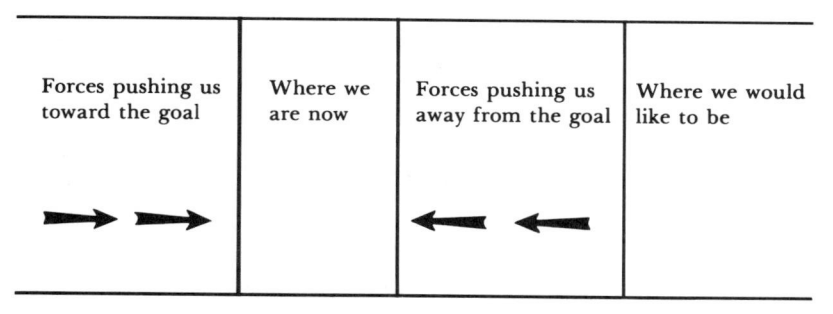

Forces pushing us toward the goal	Where we are now	Forces pushing us away from the goal	Where we would like to be
→ →		← ←	

Fig. 1. Typical chart for entering force-field information.

It is a mistake to limit involvement in problem identification and problem-solving activities to only the school staff. Parents, citizen groups, and students can be very helpful in developing a program and can exert considerable influence in assuring that the program is protected from attack from either outside or inside the school system.

Any group that is involved in the early stages is likely to become committed to the endeavor, especially if there is satisfaction and status gained from being identified with it. Once committed, these groups become a constituency that may be expected to fight for the program. Frequently during the initial stages of establishing a successful school program, it is endangered from both malicious and unintended pressures. The constituency is invaluable at such times. Of course, the staff is a constituency if it is involved, but staffs do not have the power that other groups may have against such forces as the school board, or the legislature, or local gossip.

But political protection is not the only reason for involving other groups. They can play important and sometimes irreplaceable roles for implementing change. Most of the schools in the survey involved nonprofessional staff, students, parents and community members in the life of the school. Parents can offer ideas for addressing problems and can provide many useful services. Nonprofessional staff can make important contributions to total school operation, and they can have strong influence on community opinions.

If one were to identify a single resource or the most ideally suited source for achieving better discipline and better achievement in American public schools, it would be the students themselves. Their responsible participation can do more to improve the life of the school than any other group can. The experiences reported by the schools in our survey serve to prove the value of student involvement.

The Northwest Regional Laboratory has developed materials for training school staffs to use interpersonal communications skills, along with brainstorming and force-field analysis, to identify problems and to find solutions. The methods are described in detail in two structured inservice packets titled IPC (Interpersonal Communications) and *RUPS* (Research Using Problem-Solving Techniques), which may be obtained from the Laboratory if they are not available at a local college or university.*

Step 3. *Specify how you will know when you have reached your goal.* Problem solvers must have a clear idea of what things will look like if they are successful. Most statements of educational goals are so vague or general that staff often do not know whether a goal is attained or not. The staff need some clear *indicators* that will be tangible evidence of success. If the staff can answer the question, "What would a stranger see happening in our school if we are successful in making the change we want to make?" then they will have a specific idea of what their goal means in practice.

Step 4. *Select a change strategy that is compatible with the norms and traditions of your school.* School norms and traditions govern what people do, what they believe, and what they value. They are often unspoken and people may even be unconscious of them. Only experience, keen observation, and careful listening will uncover them; but they are strong and difficult to challenge or to change. When you set out to improve a school, you are dealing with an organization as well as teaching the people within it to do new things, to think new thoughts, and to relate to one another in new ways. Violating a school's norms and traditions can set you back or even scuttle your plan; so you are well-advised to know what these norms are.

The strength of organizational traditions may be seen in our experience with a school in a large Midwestern city where a new principal was determined to make life easier for the teachers in the hope that they would devote more time to improving instruction for the inner-city Appalachian and black children who attended the school. He assigned all extracurricular activities to

---

*Northwest Regional Education Laboratory, 710 S.W. Second Avenue, Portland, Oregon, 97204. (503) 224-3650.

volunteers or to younger staff members who had not yet "paid their dues," as he saw it. The staff and the students were in chaos as a result of his efforts. A 25-year veteran transferred from the school and explained her dissatisfaction with this telling remark, "For years I've waited to become the oldest teacher on the staff so I would get to direct the Christmas pageant; then he comes along and gives it to one of the newest teachers in the building."

Seymour Sarason calls such traditions and habits the "constitution" that silently controls the activities in a school. His book, *The Culture of the School and the Problem of Change* (Allyn and Bacon, 1971) is quite helpful for analyzing a school and its culture. The chapters on the teacher and the classroom are also helpful for anyone who wants to understand behavior in a particular classroom.

Of course, there may be some norms and traditions in the school that you cannot condone or that you feel are harmful to the goals you wish to achieve. Don't challenge any that you don't have to. Adapt your plan to accommodate those that do no serious harm or that you cannot change.

Be sensitive to what leadership style is currently best suited to the school. Determine whether your staff is ready for group problem solving or whether it is better to approach them with fairly well-developed proposals and a plan of action. Even though we advocate participative methods throughout this *Handbook* because they yield long-lasting improvement, these methods must be learned. People start learning from where they are; so it is important to begin with an approach that is in tune with their previous experience. For example, in a school with a democratic environment, you can enlist the staff's participation very early by asking them to list the problems and state the goals; but a staff without experience in democratic problem solving might have to be approached with a prepared list of problems or a prepared list of goals or even a prepared list of solutions, which they could be asked to pare down or to add to.

Begin by asking yourself two questions: 1) What is the current method for making decisions in the school? 2) How satisfied is the staff with the method? If the staff is satisfied with the current method, regardless of whether it involves broad staff participation, it is probably better to begin with that method. Schools tend to go in cycles from broad staff participation to more authoritarian approaches. Neither style is necessarily "good" or "bad"; they are simply the nature of normal cycles of organizational life. Both high and low participative approaches to problem solving have positive and negative consequences as is shown in Table 10. When the staff becomes sufficiently "fed up" with the negative consequences of one, it would be best to begin with the other. Although it is the commission's view that school leaders should work toward greater staff involvement in decision making, the process for achieving that goal must be in tune with the staff's current operational style.

Step 5. *Use techniques that will help people to learn those skills necessary for reinforcing and sustaining change as well as to prepare them for participating in continuing problem solving.* Bringing about the change in a school requires more than simply initiating a new practice; it requires establishing new habits that will supplant existing ones that do not seem to be as productive. Failure to recognize this often leads to superficial changes and to short-lived practices. For example, setting up a new system of meting out punishments for fighting in school leads to far less permanent change than if we set out to establish behaviors that provide better ways to settle interpersonal or intergroup differences. The latter may take longer to achieve, but it will result in a more fundamental change in the school, because staff and students have learned a new set of operations rather than merely obeying a new set of dictates.

The techniques presented throughout this *Handbook* are based on an approach that educates staff, students, and parents to engage in ongoing problem solving in school and out of school. An investment in teaching problem-solving skills begins to yield results in later endeavors. Problems get resolved as a matter of course and fewer new ones arise.

Step 6. *Win trust and confidence from those who must help you to reach the goal.* Trust is difficult to win and easy to lose. Some change can be brought about by forcing others to do what you want them to, but such changes seldom last. Even in schools where staff expect to obey authority figures, the principal can rely for only a short time on using power alone. Generally, people who rely upon coercion to effect change work against the types of changes we found in the schools in our survey.

The means for winning trust are highly idiosyncratic to each situation, but those who want to effect change must know that trust does not automatically come with a promotion or that being "right" is not enough to enlist the support of others, particularly if people are asked to change their personal behavior.

TABLE 10

ADVANTAGES AND DISADVANTAGES OF HIGH AND LOW PARTICIPATIVE PROBLEM-SOLVING APPROACHES

Method	Advantages	Disadvantages
High Participative	Promotes wider understanding of problem.	Takes more time.
	Participants feel they own the solution.	Requires lots of meetings.
	Process addresses felt problems.	Dissipates responsibility.
	Assures more on-site attention to solving problems.	Leads to "group think," which discourages new ideas.
	Information is disseminated to more people who must carry out solutions.	Requires more from staff.
	Participants take more responsibility.	Discourages task-oriented personnel.
	Builds confidence and pride in participants.	Leads to demands for more centralized decision making.
	Spreads skills among staff.	
	Takes pressure off "bosses" to hide problems.	
Low Participative	Takes less time to formulate decisions.	Fewer people feel responsible for decisions.
	Takes less energy from group.	Leads to "Let George do it" attitudes.
	Focuses responsibility for decisions on the originator.	Reduces number of people who have skills.
	Permits "boss" to decide what to do.	Discourages problem identification and creative solutions.
	Preserves authority ladder.	Centralizes decisions that others would like to make or should make.
	Overcomes the group habit of hiding problems.	Leads to demands for more participation.

Trust is won by making good decisions, by helping others achieve their goals, by involving others in planning. Do your homework, be open to suggestions, and above all, be consistent. Do your own work well before suggesting that others do theirs differently. Show that you can get things done. Trust is developed in the interactions among staff that occur while the goals and plans are being developed, particularly if those interactions make every participant feel involved and respected.

Step 7. *Make a list of those people who have to know about the change and "sell" it to them.* Generally, the people who have to know about a change are those who have to work to make it happen and those who must supply resources essential for its success.

It helps to have friends in high places inside the organization. The assistant superintendent, a supervisor, or the secretaries in the personnel office or the curriculum development office can all be helpful in the same ways that other constituencies are. Staff in good schools keep their fences mended in the important decision centers and supply centers in the district.

Those who have to know must be told and they must be "sold." They are more easily sold if they have a reason to trust the person or group that is initiating the change. Marshal all the evidence you can that the problem you want to resolve is a problem for the people you are trying to sell. They are much more likely to support it if they feel they will benefit.

Too many good programs founder because the staff is unprepared to explain them and sell them to parents. Parents are naturally interested in new practices that will benefit their children; but if they can't learn what a new practice is all about or can't be persuaded that it will benefit their children, they may organize to get rid of the new practice. School staff should not begin any new practice without expecting to *teach* parents what it is, why it is, and what value it has for them and their children.

Step 8. *Give the project a name or a title in order to give people a way of identifying with it and for communicating about it.* People seem to like to be associated with a program that is distinctive and has its own identity. They also seem to need some shorthand way of communicating about it. Witness the proliferation of names and acronyms used for federal and foundation education projects over the past two decades. Many of the schools in our survey used acronyms or catchy titles for their programs, which no doubt facilitated discussion about those programs by staff, students, parents, and community members. So they would issue "Grovers" instead of tokens or points for good work, or they would recruit students as "Bleacher Creatures" instead of asking them to cheer for the team, or they would send "Happy Grams" instead of notes to parents.

While making this recommendation, the commission does feel a word of caution is in order. Giving a program a catchy title or acronym can set it apart so much that it becomes an easy target for criticism, or it can create divisions on a staff. Giving a fancy name to a practice can generate cynicism in others who have been doing the same things for years, so they conclude that someone is trying to package an old product in a flashy new wrap. One of our authors (Wayson) feels that the demise of many federal programs was due to some extent in giving them separate identities, which made them easy targets for cutting when budgets were curtailed or when criticism mounted.

Step 9. *Hold frequent meetings to solve problems, to give people a sense of being involved, to improve communications, to monitor progress, and to keep spirits from flagging.* If a new program is to succeed, it must be discussed frequently and monitored continuously. Successful change requires frequent interaction in order to foster mutual support as the new practice takes hold and old practices are eliminated or modified. With the daily pressures of their jobs, staff naturally fall back on old practices and let new assignments or new practices slip to the "back burner." They need the stimulation and support that they get from interacting about the new practice, sharing experiences, solving problems that come up, and bolstering one another to keep trying. A Rand Corporation study found that regular meetings that focused on problem solving were a vital part of programs that succeeded and survived.*

However, many schools fail because they rely only on formal meetings with a prearranged agenda and a specific time and place. While such formal meetings are important, little improvement can occur if the only interaction provided is in formal meetings. It helps when people can talk about problems and practices and interact with one another in informal settings such as discussions in the lunchroom, chats in the teachers' lounge, or conversations over a beer or a coke after school in a nearby

---

*Paul Berman and Milbray McLaughlin, *Federal Programs Supporting Educational Change, vol. 3: Implementing and Sustaining Innovations.* Santa Monica, Calif.: The Rand Corporation, 1978.

lounge, or wherever people go to let their hair down. So the good planner will encourage informal meetings and discussions and will participate in many such meetings. One sign of a successful school program is when the people involved are discussing it and improving it in informal settings.

Step 10. *Divide the work into manageable tasks, assign and monitor specific responsibilities, and set realistic deadlines for getting the work done.* No plan is useful unless it achieves its goals, and no plan can achieve its goals until someone gets to work. We call this step in the change process "belling the cat" from the fable about the mice who decided to save their lives by putting a bell on the cat. They found the idea tremendously appealing until they tried to find someone who would put the bell on the cat. No plan is worthwhile if the group does not "bell the cat," which means deciding who will do what, by what time, and report back to whom. One reason so many good plans fall by the wayside is that the staff never take this step; they leave the faculty meetings marveling at the brilliant ideas that came up, but no one has any responsibility for doing anything between now and the next meeting.

Develop a systematic plan for getting the work done. There are many planning procedures that help. All include reasonable timelines for getting the job done. The form in Fig. 2 has been used by many schools to guide their planning. It is self-explanatory. After using the form for several different problems, participants find it quite easy to break down complex projects into tasks that are manageable.

Some authorities on planning frighten school staffs by making the whole thing seem terribly complex, but anyone who has organized a successful field trip has already demonstrated the necessary management skills. Anyone who has cooked a big Thanksgiving dinner has mastered the process of breaking down work into small tasks and assigning the tasks to be accomplished within a specified timeline. Getting the whole meal on the table at the proper temperatures at the same time is just a smaller version of what it takes to organize a parent-faculty-student cleanup day or honors assembly.

For further information on project management you may want to read Desmond Cook's *Educational Project Management*[*] or

---

[*]Desmond Cook, *Educational Project Management.* Columbus, Ohio: Charles E. Merrill, 1971.

Action Plan

Goal	Indicators of success	Activities necessary for reaching the goal	Resources needed to do the activity	Time when activity has to be done	Person responsible for doing the job

Fig. 2. Form for assigning tasks and deadlines to complete an action plan

contact Research for Better Schools* about its materials for teaching the basic principles of project management. Such skills are very useful for anyone who participates in a problem-solving approach in schools that emphasize self-discipline.

Step 11. *The group should have some early success experiences that it can celebrate.* Problem solvers must have some early identifiable successes that were achieved through cooperative effort. A success that comes about through one person's effort is not enough. Indeed, too often the success of one person only serves to reinforce the idea that someone else will do whatever needs to be done and that the rest of the staff are not responsible for addressing problems. The staff need to be able to say "We did it!" This is why it is important to start with problems that the group feels

---

*Project Management Basic Principles and Techniques is a skill-building training program designed to increase skills and knowledge for planning, operating, and terminating projects. Contact: Research for Better Schools, Suite 1700, 1700 Market St., Philadelphia, PA., 19103. (215) 561-4100, ext. 237.

are important. Even if the problem seems trivial at the time, success can come easily and in short time, giving the staff early encouragement for going on to larger, more important problems.

It is also useful to have other groups (identified in Step 7) know about the successes, but a school must proceed with caution in trumpeting success. Many schools that were nominated for our study chose not to participate because they feared that publicity would cause someone or some group in the system to undermine what they were doing. We interviewed 12 principals who had "turned schools around" in a large city, and each of them agreed that they could not have created a good school program without violating some policy, law, or contract provision. Consequently, each of them stated that they had done what they had done *quietly*. In their situations, the best rule is to hide your light if it attracts bombers.

Step 12. Institute procedures that assure continuing maintenance of the new practice and that provide follow-up and revisions. No new program in a school is ever completely installed. With new students constantly coming into the school and others leaving, with staff turnover, and with great mobility among parents, the program must be periodically evaluated, revised if necessary, and then taught to new participants.

Plan well in advance. Too many schools operate on a day-to-day agenda when they should be planning a year (or more) ahead. September is too late to do what is necessary to establish good discipline at the start of the school year. Actions to be taken should be announced by the previous March, and committees should be assigned by April and working by May if September is to go well. Events scheduled for December should be staffed and planned by October. If key members are leaving the school in June, replacements should be trained for the job months before. Therefore, build timelines and make assignments to assure the continuation of activities over any foreseeable crises or breaks.

Orienting and enlisting commitment from new people—staff, students, and parents—should be a part of any program whether new or old. New people have not participated in the experiences that led to the development of a program; they have neither the motivation of those who "knew how bad it was before" nor the commitment that comes from having been involved in solving the problem. Using staff, students, and parents to orient newcomers to the program is the best way to keep the program alive and prospering.

Maintaining the constituency that was discussed in Step 2 is vital to the maintenance of a program. The constituency helps to communicate the purposes of the program to others, helps to secure resources, and provides "friends in high places" whose help can be crucial at the least expected times. The strongest and easiest developed constituency for a school is an active, involved group of parents. Their continued involvement is the best assurance that they will be advocates for the school and its programs.

Without helpful constituencies, change efforts could be sabotaged overnight — or most certainly over a summer's vacation. Guardians of a school are most vulnerable during summer vacations because they are away, and much damage can be done through reassigning staff, cutting budgets, or withholding resources.

6
Conclusion and a Caution

Following the principles and steps presented in this *Handbook* cannot assure success, but they can help to avoid the most common mistakes that school planners make; and they do suggest corrective mechanisms that can help when mistakes are made or when the going gets rough.

From what we know about change and innovation in education, a word of caution is appropriate: *Effective educational programs are ephemeral.* In these times even good programs are vulnerable, so they often have very short lives unless there are continuing infusions of creativity, energy, and enthusiasm. Don Everitt, experienced school principal from the Cincinnati area, nominated several schools in the survey, but commented,

> I truly believe that good school discipline is basically dependent upon the combined thinking and activities of a majority of parents, school personnel, and students. It is, therefore, obvious that a sharp break in thinking and/or activities can destroy the stability of a good school discipline atmosphere.

Even if staff and community remain stable — a rare event even in rural areas — effective programs demand more from school personnel in the way of commitment and energy than is standard in many hierarchically organized, large centralized school districts. The difference is so great that few can sustain such expenditure of energy for long periods, as is illustrated in a story that appeared in the *Cincinnati Post* (14 February 1980) titled "How a Model School Can Go Astray." The article described a school which five years before had been "a decidedly positive school . . . with relatively high marks on the 1974 statewide assessment tests — scores usually associated with schools in middle-class areas

. . . although many of its students came from low-income families."

> But something has happened to this elementary school . . . Today, the observer who spends some time in Edison's classrooms and talking with its staff and students might well wonder if he had stumbled into the wrong school.
>
> Edison has the same principal. Teacher turnover has been low. Its students come from the same kinds of backgrounds, and their achievement scores are about the same. But almost everyone of the positive attributes identified by the university researchers is no longer to be found at Edison.

The article goes on to show how an exciting program with an enthusiastic and caring staff drifted into mediocrity, cynicism, and low morale. A formerly active parent states, "Other schools are for kids; this one is not. They don't give a damn at that school."

The reporter petulantly blames the principal for the loss of a dream but sheds no light on what happened to bring about the decline in the school. Nor is there any indication that the university researchers have delved into its causes. But the story echoes what has happened to many school improvement efforts in the face of a fast-paced and impersonal technological society. Good schools are hard to come by and even harder to sustain. Perhaps it is inevitable that in a throw-away world of planned obsolescence, effective educational programs will be transitory. The proposition deserves prompt and thorough attention from researchers, planners, and innovators before the public schools become an endangered species, breathing their last gasp.

The message for educators is threefold: 1) providing good education for even short periods is worthwhile in itself; 2) don't retire from your job thinking you have built a program that will last forever; and 3) plan and institute ways to renew the program and to sustain it through such foreseeable exigencies as a change in principal, staff turnover, decline in resources, or changes in school board composition.

Bibliography

American Friends Service Committee. *Creative Discipline: Searching For the Better Way.* Newsletter Series. Columbia, S.C.: Southeastern Public Education Program, 1977-1978.

Berne, Eric. *Transactional Analysis in Psychotherapy: A Systematic Individual and Social Psychiatry.* New York: Grove Press, 1961.

Berne, Eric. *Games People Play: The Psychology of Human Relationships.* New York: Grove Press, 1964.

Brodinsky, Ben. *Student Discipline: Problems And Solutions.* Arlington, Va.: American Association of School Administrators, 1980.

Brundage, Diane, ed. *The Journalism Research Fellows Report: What Makes an Effective School?* Washington, D.C.: The George Washington University's Institute for Educational Leadership, 1980.

Canter, Lee, and Canter, Marlene. *Assertive Discipline: A Take Charge Approach For Today's Educator.* Los Angeles: Canter and Associates, Inc., 1976.

Dreikurs, Rudolf, and Cassel, Pearl. *Discipline Without Tears.* New York: Hawthorne Books, 1974.

Ellis, Albert. *Humanistic Psychotherapy: The Rational-Emotive Approach.* New York: Julian Press, 1973.

Ellis, Albert and Harper, Robert A. *A New Guide to Rational Living.* North Hollywood, Calif.: Wilshire Book Company, 1979.

First, Joan McCarty, and Mizell, M. Hayes, eds. *Everybody's Business: A Book About School Discipline.* Columbia, S.C.: Southeastern Public Education Program, 1980.

Glasser, William. *Reality Therapy, A New Approach to Psychiatry.* New York: Harper and Row, 1965.

———. *Schools Without Failure.* New York: Harper and Row, 1969.

Gordon, Thomas. *P.E.T.: Parent Effectiveness Training.* New York: New American Library, 1970.

Gordon, Thomas, and Burch, Noel. *T.E.T.: Teacher Effectiveness Training.* New York: Peter H. Wyden Books, 1974.

Harris, Thomas. *I'm OK—You're OK.* New York: Harper and Row, 1967.

Howard, Eugene R. *School Discipline Desk Book.* West Nyack, N.Y.: Parker, 1978.

Hunter, Madeline. *Reinforcement Theory for Teachers: A Programmed Book.* El Segundo, Calif.: TIP Publications, 1967.

———. *Motivation Theory for Teachers: A Programmed Book.* El Segundo, Calif.: TIP Publications, 1967.

———. *Retention Theory for Teachers: A Programmed Book.* El Segundo, Calif.: TIP Publications, 1967.

———. *Teach for Transfer: A Programmed Book.* El Segundo, Calif.: TIP Publications, 1971.

Improved Instruction. El Segundo, Calif.: TIP Publications, 1976.

Kaeser, Susan C. *Orderly Schools That Serve All Children: A Review of Successful Schools in Ohio.* Cleveland, Ohio: Citizens' Council for Ohio Schools, 1979.

Milgram, Stanley. *Obedience to Authority.* New York: Harper and Row, 1974.

National Diffusion Network. *Educational Programs That Work.* San Francisco, Calif.: Far West Laboratory for Educational Research and Development, 1980.

———. "Positive Alternatives to Student Suspensions (PASS): A Validated Pupil Personnel Services Demonstration Project." In *Educational Programs That Work.* San Francisco, Calif.: Far West Laboratory for Educational Research and Development, 1980.

Phi Delta Kappa. *Why Do Some Urban Schools Succeed? The Phi Delta Kappa Study of Exemplary Urban Elementary Schools.* Bloomington, Ind.: Phi Delta Kappa, 1980.

Purkey, William W. *Self-Concept and School Achievement.* Englewood Cliffs, N.J.: Prentice-Hall, 1970.

———. *Inviting School Success.* Belmont, Calif.: Wadsworth, 1978.

Silberman, Melvin L., and Wheelan, Susan A. *How To Discipline Without Feeling Guilty.* New York: Hawthorne Books, 1980.

Wayson, William W., and Pinnell, Gay Su. "Developing Discipline With Quality Schools." *Citizen Guide to Quality Education*. Cleveland, Ohio: Citizens' Council for Ohio Schools, 1978.

Wolfgang, Charles H., and Glickman, Carl D. *Solving Discipline Problems: Strategies For Classroom Teachers.* Boston: Allyn and Bacon, 1980.

Wynne, Edward A. *Looking At Schools: Good, Bad, and Indifferent.* Lexington, Mass.: Lexington Books, 1980.